Peru

Peru

BY MICHAEL BURGAN

Enchantment of the World™
Second Series

CHILDREN'S PRESS®

An Imprint of Scholastic Inc.

Frontispiece: **San Francisco Church, Lima**

Consultant: Robert Austin, PhD, Associate Professor, Centre for European, Russian and Eurasian Studies, University of Toronto, Toronto, Ontario

Please note: All statistics are as up-to-date as possible at the time of publication.

Book production by The Design Lab

Library of Congress Cataloging-in-Publication Data
Names: Burgan, Michael, author.
Title: Peru / by Michael Burgan.
Description: New York, NY : Children's Press, an Imprint of Scholastic, 2018.
  | Series: Enchantment of the world | Includes bibliographical references
  and index.
Identifiers: LCCN 2017028549 | ISBN 9780531235911 (library binding)
Subjects: LCSH: Peru—Juvenile literature.
Classification: LCC F3408.5 .B87 2018 | DDC 985—dc23
LC record available at https://lccn.loc.gov/2017028549

Scholastic Inc., 557 Broadway, New York, NY 10012

1 2 3 4 5 6 7 8 9 10 R 27 26 25 24 23 22 21 20 19 18

Mount Chicón

Contents

Left to right:
Canopy walk, traditional clothing, sandboarding, floating islands, macaws

CHAPTER 1

Ancient Cultures, Diverse Land

THE SOUTH AMERICAN NATION OF PERU HAS AN amazing array of landscapes and climates. Beaches, snow-capped mountains, humid jungles, dry deserts—Peru has them all, in a country slightly smaller than the state of Alaska.

Small rivers that start in the towering Andes Mountains of Peru are the source of the world's second-longest river, the Amazon. The Peruvian rain forests near the river are home to thousands of different kinds of plants and animals, many found nowhere else on earth. The remote jungles are also home to small groups of people who live mostly cut off from the rest of the world. In Spanish, one of Peru's three official languages, they are called *aislados*—"isolated people." They have chosen to live separate from outsiders, and hunt and fish much as their ancestors did centuries ago. They are just some of Peru's indigenous population—ethnic groups whose ancestors lived in the country before Europeans arrived.

Opposite: **A woman paddles a boat across Lake Titicaca, which lies high in the Andes Mountains. It is the largest lake in South America.**

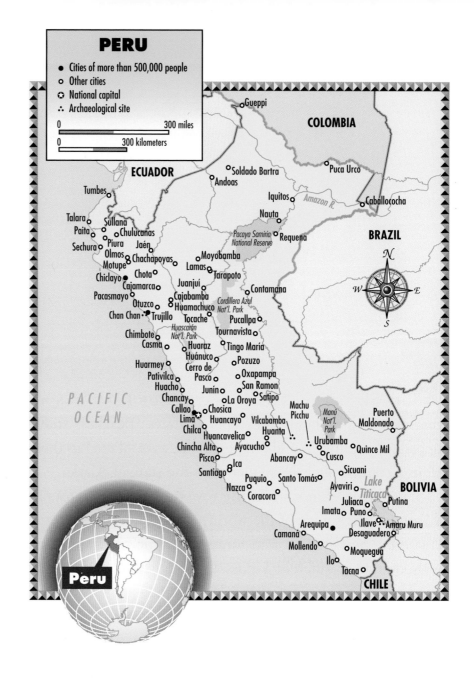

PERU

- Cities of more than 500,000 people
- Other cities
- National capital
- Archaeological site

0   300 miles

0   300 kilometers

COLOMBIA

Gueppi

Soldado Bartra

Andoas

Puca Urco

ECUADOR

Tumbes

Iquitos   Amazon R.   Caballococha

Nauta

Talara

Sullana

Requena   BRAZIL

Paita   Chulucanas

Pacaya Samiria

Sechura   Piura   Jaén   National Reserve

Olmos   Chachapoyas   Moyobamba

Motupe   Lamas   Tarapoto

Chiclayo   Chota

Cajamarca   Juanjuí   Contamana

Pacasmayo   Cajabamba

Otuzco   Huamachuco   Cordillera Azul   N

Chan Chan   Trujillo   Tocache   Nat'l. Park

Huascarán   Pucallpa   W   E

Chimbote   Nat'l. Park   Tournavista

Casma   Huaraz   Tingo María   S

Huánuco

Huarmey   Cerro de   Pozuzo

Pativilca   Pasco   Oxapampa

Huacho   Junín   San Ramon

Chancay   La Oroya   Satipo

Callao   Chosica   Machu   Puerto

Lima   Huancayo   Picchu   Manú   Maldonado

Chilca   Vilcabamba   Nat'l.

Huancavelica   Huanta   Park   Urubamba   Quince Mil

Chincha Alta   Ayacucho   Cusco

Pisco   Abancay   Sicuani

Santiago   Ica   Ayaviri   Lake

Nazca   Puquio   Santo Tomás   Titicaca   BOLIVIA

Coracora   Juliaca   Putina

Imata   Puno

Arequipa   Ilave   Amaru Muru

Camaná   Desaguadero

Mollendo   Moquegua

Ilo

Tacna   CHILE

PACIFIC OCEAN

Peru

One of Peru's most notable natural landmarks is Lake Titicaca, which the country shares with Bolivia. It is the largest lake in South America. In the region around the lake, people first raised the potato as a crop, and it is still an important part of meals eaten across Peru. Farmers raise about four thousand different kinds of potatoes there.

The Rise and Fall of Empires

Taking wild plants and animals and raising them on farms is a process called domestication. Ancient Peruvians first raised several crops now grown in other countries, including quinoa, a grain, and cotton, which is used to make clothing. The development of farming helped lead to the creation of different civilizations in what became Peru. The Inca Empire was

In Peru, potatoes come in many shapes, colors, and sizes.

Becoming a Modern Nation

Since becoming independent, the country has sometimes been ruled by military leaders who seized power rather than winning elections. Poverty has also remained a problem, in both rural areas and in parts of the major cities. Starting in the 1980s, two major rebel groups tried to use violence to stir up fear and take control of the government. The rebels failed to gain power, but tens of thousands of people died in the years it took to quash the rebellion.

A girl stands by a row of shacks in her town in northern Peru. Poor people in Peru have to make their homes out of whatever scrap metal or wood they can find.

Teenagers play in a fountain in Tacna, a thriving city in southern Peru.

In the twenty-first century, Peru's leaders have worked hard to improve education and the economy. The country has also done more to promote the rights of the Quechua and other native peoples, though at times they have fought with the government over control of their lands.

Despite its recent troubles, Peru continues to make progress in making life better for people across its diverse regions. After being elected president in 2016, Pedro Pablo Kuczynski said he wanted to build a country that was "more modern, more just, more equal." As he and the rest of the country attempt to do that, Peru attracts travelers from around the world. They come to explore the country's natural beauty, diverse wildlife, and the wonders left behind by the Incas and others.

CHAPTER 2

A Land of Contrasts

WALKING ALONG PERU'S PACIFIC COAST, YOU might feel a cool mist on your skin from fog rolling in off the ocean. Head east, and the snowy peaks of the Andes rise above the coastal plain. Then, beyond the massive mountain range is the Amazon rain forest, where rain and humidity shape the region.

The geographically diverse land of Peru sits on the western coast of South America, just south of the equator, which divides earth into the Northern and Southern Hemispheres. Peru also claims part of Antarctica as its territory.

Geographers usually divide Peru into three main regions. Within each of the three regions, Peru has a wide range of geographic features.

Jagged ridges break up the desert in southern Peru.

The Coastal Plain

Peru's Pacific coastline is about 1,500 miles (2,400 kilometers) long. It makes up just 11 percent of the country's area but it is home to slightly more than half of its population. In some places, this mostly flat region extends up to 100 miles (160 km) into Peru's interior. The coastal plain has some fertile farmland, fed by melting snow from the Andes that fills rivers that run to the ocean. But the Sechura Desert covers most of the region. It is the site of the Cerro Blanco sand dune, one of the largest in the world, which reaches almost 4,000 feet (1,200 meters) high.

A Look at Peru's Cities

Lima, the capital of Peru, is by far its largest city, with an estimated population of 7,737,002 in 2017. Arequipa is Peru's second-largest city, home to 841,130. Located in southern Peru, it earned the nickname the White City because many of its buildings are made from white volcanic rock. Three volcanoes overlook the city, and it has often experienced damaging earthquakes. That led people to keep their buildings low and solid, to help them survive the quakes. The site of the city had been occupied for thousands of years when the Spanish arrived there in 1540. Some Spanish colonial buildings still stand today, including the Santa Catalina Monastery (above right). This monastery, still home to some nuns, was founded in 1580. Another popular tourist attraction is the Museum of Andean Sanctuaries. This museum houses Incan mummies found on Ampato, a dormant volcano, as well as items once used by Incas. Arequipa is southern Peru's major economic center. It has many factories and an active tourist industry.

Peru's third-largest city, Callao, is home to 813,264

people. Located right next to Lima, it is the country's main seaport. The city was founded in 1537, and as a major port it suffered frequent attacks by pirates and others. In the 1700s, a large fortress was constructed to protect the city, and it still stands. Today, Callao is home to a large military base and Peru's main airport.

Located on Peru's northern coast, Trujillo is Peru's fourth-largest city, with a population of 747,450. Francisco Pizarro, who conquered the Incas, named the city for his hometown in Spain. Like other parts of Peru, Trujillo often experiences strong earthquakes. One in 1619 destroyed the entire city, but the Spanish rebuilt it. Many colonial buildings line Trujillo's main square, the Plaza de Armas (left). One of these is the cathedral, which was built in 1666. Today, Trujillo draws many surfers to the nearby beaches.

Just north of Trujillo along the Pacific coast is Chiclayo. With a population of 577,375, it's Peru's fifth-largest city. Founded by the Spanish in 1560, Chiclayo remained just a small village for several hundred years. Several museums in Chiclayo display some of the riches found in the tombs of Moche, an ancient people who lived nearby. Some of these artifacts are more than 1,500 years old. These artifacts, which include gold and silver items, help historians understand how the Moche lived.

Peru's Geographic Features

Area: 496,224 square miles (1,285,214 sq km)

Highest Elevation: Huascarán, 22,205 feet (6,768 m) above sea level

Lowest Elevation: Bayóvar Depression, 111 feet (34 m) below sea level

Longest River: Ucayali, about 990 miles (1,600 km)

Largest Lake: Titicaca (shared with Bolivia), 3,232 square miles (8,371 sq km)

Highest Lake: Titicaca, 12,500 feet (3,810 m)

Highest Active Volcano: Sabancaya, 19,572 feet (5,966 m) above sea level

Deepest Canyon: Cotahuasi (below), 11,598 feet (3,535 m)

Highest Recorded Temperature: 108°F (42°C) in Pucallpa

Lowest Recorded Temperature: -13°F (-25°C) in Imata

Average Daily High Temperature: In Lima, 82°F (28°C) in February, 66°F (19°C) in July; in Cusco, 64.5°F (18°C) in February, 64.5°F (18°C) in July

Average Daily Low Temperature: In Lima, 65°F (18.5°C) in February, 54°F (12°C) in July; in Cusco, 43°F (6°C) in February, 32°F (0°C) in July

Average Annual Precipitation: Varies, from 0.3 inches (0.8 cm) in Lima to 198 inches (503 cm) in Quince Mil

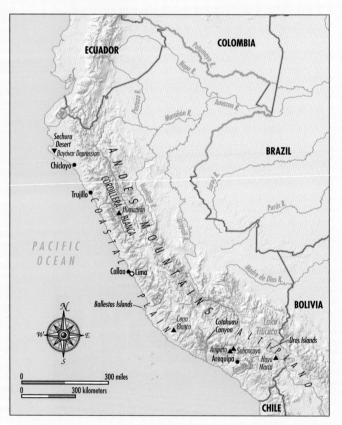

The Highlands

East of the coastal regions is Peru's highlands. The land here gradually begins to increase in elevation before reaching its greatest height in the Peruvian Andes. One section of these mountains is the Cordillera Blanca, or White Range, which includes Huascarán. At 22,205 feet (6,768 m), this peak is the highest spot in Peru. The snowcapped Cordillera Blanca also has glaciers that melted to form lakes. These are the world's highest glaciers in the tropics, the region surrounding the equator, but scientists warn they could disappear by 2055 as earth warms in a process called climate change.

To the west of the Andes in southern Peru is a region called the altiplano, or high plain. This region has an average

The Andes are one of the world's great mountain ranges. They run all the way from the northern coast of South America to the continent's southern tip.

Plates Beneath the Earth

Massive plates of rock, called tectonic plates, lie below earth's surface and its oceans. These plates sometimes shift. Long ago, a plate under the Pacific Ocean moved underneath another plate, pushing up land and creating the Andes. The movement of tectonic plates still affects Peru today. Peru sits along the Ring of Fire, a U-shaped region on the edge of most of the Pacific Ocean that experiences many of the world's earthquakes. These quakes are caused by plate movement. In 1970 Peru experienced its deadliest natural disaster ever when an earthquake centered in Chimbote killed seventy thousand people. The Ring of Fire also has many active volcanoes. Peru has several, and in 2016, two of them, just 60 miles (100 km) apart, erupted at the same time.

elevation of about 11,000 feet (3,350 m). It features what is said to be the deepest canyon in the world, Cotahuasi. It is almost twice as deep as Arizona's Grand Canyon. At the

The Floating Islands of Titicaca

One of the most famous sights on Lake Titicaca is its floating islands. Called the Uros Islands, they are made out of reeds that grow in the lake. The local people, the Uros, built them hundreds of years ago to escape attack from invading forces, including the Incas. The Uros used the reeds to make floating mats that are about 12 feet (4 m) thick. Today, dozens of the islands still exist, and the Uros have their own communities that include schools and small stores. Most supplies reach the islands by boat, and tourists can visit some of the islands.

The Doorway to Nowhere

Not far from Lake Titicaca is a stone wall that has puzzled scientists. The rock has been smoothed at the bottom, and someone carved what looks like a doorway into the thick, red stone. The doorway, though, does not go all the way through to the other side. The rock doorway is called Amaru Muru, which is said to be the name of an Inca priest. In one legend, he vanished through the doorway to escape people who were chasing him. Local people call the hill where Amaru Muru sits Hayu Marca, "gate of the spirits." Legends in the region talk about seeing mysterious beings emerging from the doorway. Some people have claimed they have passed through it into other worlds. Who carved the doorway and why remains a mystery. One theory is that it was a building project that the Incas never completed.

southern end of the altiplano is Lake Titicaca, which Peru shares with the neighboring country of Bolivia. It's the largest lake in South America, measured by the amount of water it holds. And sitting at an elevation of 12,500 feet (3,810 m), it's the highest lake in the world that boats can use. According to an Inca legend, the first humans emerged from this lake.

The Amazon Region

More than half of Peru is made up of the *selva*, or the country's Amazon region. This region east of the Amazon is about the size of California. It includes hills sloping down from the Andes, forests, grasslands, and rain forests. It has two distinct areas. The northern part receives more rain and is often

Mining Brings Problems

Mining can cause damage to the environment even when it's done legally. But in Peru's Amazon rain forest, illegal mining for gold has created severe problems. The miners cut down large areas of trees, then sift through the soil for tiny flecks of gold. The miners not only destroy the soil, but they leave behind mercury, a poisonous material used to process the gold. In 2016, tests done on nearby villagers showed their bodies had taken in high levels of mercury, which can cause kidney damage in adults and brain damage in children. The illegal mining also destroys the environment. The Peruvian government tries to arrest people mining illegally, but it is hard to do when they can mine in such a large and remote area.

flooded, while the southern part is drier. Many parts of Peru's selva are protected from being developed, as the government has created several national parks there. One of the largest is Manú National Park, which is thought to be the region with the greatest variety of plant and animal life on earth.

Climate

Just as Peru's landscape varies greatly, so does its climate. Even within one geographic region, the climate is not the same everywhere. In the coastal region, for example, the northern part is usually sunny and humid, with almost no rain. The central and southern parts are not as warm as the north, and they get more clouds. All along the coast, fog often forms during winter. In Peru, the seasons are the opposite of what they are in North America, so winter comes between June and August, and the summer is from December to February. During the summer, Lima has an average high temperature of around 85 degrees Fahrenheit (29 degrees Celsius). The winter high there is about 70°F (21°C). The climate along the coast is shaped in part by the Peru Current, which carries cold water up from Antarctica along the Pacific coast of South America. This current brings Peru's coast its winter fog but also limits rainfall there.

Manú National Park protects a thriving rain forest habitat. More than 300 inches (800 cm) of rain fall in some parts of the park each year.

A man steers a boat on Los Amigos River in the Amazon region. Some rivers in the Amazon are important transportation routes.

Much of the altiplano and Andes receive more precipitation, with most of it coming during the summer. Arequipa, though, on the western edge of the region, has a desertlike climate, averaging less than 4 inches (10 centimeters) of rain every year. At higher elevations, the precipitation falls as snow. Winters tend to be sunny and dry, with pleasant temperatures.

As in the highlands, the Amazon region has a long rainy season during the summer. But even during the "dry season," rain still occurs. The weather in the Amazon region is usually warm and humid, though some areas have cold stretches, when the temperature can fall to as low as 46°F (8°C).

El Niño and Peru

During the nineteenth century, fishers along Peru's Pacific coast noticed that a warm current of water sometimes headed south from the equator. When this happened, heavy rains and flooding also occurred. Since it usually happened around Christmas, the fishers named this event El Niño—the Spanish name for the baby Jesus. Today, scientists know that a particularly strong El Niño can affect the weather over large parts of the world that border the Pacific Ocean, including the United States. In Peru in 2017, heavy rains associated with El Niño led to some of the worst flooding there in several decades. The rain also caused destructive mudslides. Some scientists think a general warming of all the world's oceans may have also added to the heavy rains. The extreme weather killed more than a hundred people and led to more than $6 billion in damage.

Boys play soccer in the rain in a remote village in the Amazon. Rain is common throughout the year in the region.

CHAPTER 3

Amazing Life

THE AMAZON RAIN FOREST OF PERU IS FAMOUS for the variety of its wildlife. Scientists call this variety biodiversity. Manú National Park alone has about one thousand different kinds of birds, and many of them are endemic to Peru, meaning they are found nowhere else on earth. The park is also home to more than two hundred kinds of mammals. Its plants include at least two thousand different species, and probably many more.

But the Amazon is not the only part of Peru with breathtaking wildlife. Given its geographic diversity, Peru has interesting animals and plants all over the country. In the Andes, some smaller relatives of camels roam in the wild, while others are raised for their wool. Off the coast, the Peru Current carries tiny creatures that provide food for a variety of fish, and sea lions and seals live on islands off Peru's southern coast. Lovers of wildlife have much to explore when visiting Peru.

Opposite: **Red-and-green macaws are one of the many bird species found in Manú National Park. One of the largest parrots, the macaws grow about 3 feet (1 m) long from the top of their head to the tip of their tail.**

The jaguar is a powerful hunter. Sometimes it stalks animals in long grass. Other times, it waits in trees to ambush prey.

In the Forests and Mountains

In Peru's Amazon region lives the biggest wild cat in the Americas, the jaguar. From their noses to the tips of their tails, jaguars can reach 9 feet (2.7 m) in length. They are the largest meat-eating animals in South America. Other big cats found in Peru include the puma and the ocelot.

Sharing Peru's jungles with the big cats are dozens of kinds of primates. This animal family includes apes and monkeys. The primates of Peru are generally small, and some of them are endemic to the country. One of these is the yellow-tailed woolly monkey. It was once thought to be extinct, but scientists rediscovered some during the 1970s. Today, they are considered

National Animal: Vicuña

The vicuña is related to the llama. Although vicuñas live in the wild, Peruvians round them up to shear their wool. In Incan times, only royal people were allowed to wear clothing made from this wool. Now, anyone can—if they can afford it. Vicuña wool is one of the world's most expensive fabrics. A man's jacket can cost $21,000! Peruvians shear the wool in a ceremony called a *chacu*. A large group of people circles the animals, closing in on the vicuñas until they get close enough to cut the wool. Then the vicuñas are allowed to return to the wild.

an endangered species, which means they could be wiped out forever as humans push into the areas where they live.

In Peru's mountains and highlands live four different camelids—relatives of the camel. The largest of them is the

Yellow-tailed woolly monkeys live in the cloud forests of Peru. Their diet consists mainly of leaves, fruits, and flowers.

A Hairless Helper

For several thousand years, a tiny hairless dog has been part of daily life in Peru. Once wild, the Peruvian hairless dog was eventually tamed and became a popular pet before the rise of the Inca Empire. These dogs are also called Peruvian Inca orchids, because the Spanish often found them in caves where orchids grew. In early times, when the dogs died, people buried them with cloth and food, so they would be comfortable as they traveled to the world thought to exist for the dead. The breed almost disappeared during colonial times, but in recent years Peruvians have once again welcomed them as pets. Many people love to hug the Peruvian Inca orchids because their lack of hair makes them feel even warmer than other dogs.

llama, which can reach 6 feet (1.8 m) tall. Peru's native people domesticated the llama more than six thousand years ago and used them to carry goods through the mountains. Llamas are still used in that way today. A slightly smaller, domesticated relative of the llama is the alpaca. These animals are raised for their soft wool, which is used to make clothing. Peru's two wild camelids are the vicuña and the guanaco. Guanacos are the rarest of the four camelids. They are sometimes hunted for their meat.

A rare mammal that lives in the region between the high Andes peaks and the Amazon is the spectacled bear. It is the only bear that lives in South America. Its name comes from the rings around the eyes that some of the bears have, which look a little like eyeglasses, or spectacles.

In the Rivers and Oceans

Peru's rivers are home to several unusual animals. The giant river otter, the largest otter in the world, lives in the rivers of the Amazon, where it hunts fish. These otters can be as long as an adult man is tall. Peru also has a kind of dolphin that lives in rivers. Often called the pink dolphin because of its color, the Amazon River dolphin is the largest freshwater dolphin in the world. It can reach a length of 8 feet (2.4 m).

A giant reptile found in Peru's rivers is the anaconda. These snakes can reach 30 feet (9 m) long and weigh 500 pounds (230 kilograms). They eat a range of animals—including jaguars!

The giant river otter is about twice the length of the North American otter. It is well adapted to life in the water. It has webbed feet, as well as nostrils and ears that close up when it swims.

A Deadly Amphibian

Amphibians include frogs, toads, and salamanders. One well-known Peruvian amphibian is the poison dart frog. As its name suggests, these frogs carry a potent poison. Native hunters of the Amazon region once took the frogs' poison and put it on the tips of their arrows. The poison is one of the deadliest known. Scientists study the poison to see if it might be useful in medicine.

The piranha has an unusually powerful bite. It has a strong jaw and sharp, serrated teeth.

They wrap themselves around their food until it dies or else hold it underwater until it drowns. Then the anacondas swallow the animals whole. Other river reptiles include turtles and lizards of all kinds and the black caiman, a type of crocodile.

A Peruvian fish with a bad reputation is the piranha. Though piranhas' lower jaws are filled with sharp teeth, native people of the Amazon swim near these fish and are rarely bothered by them. Piranhas will, however, feed off of dead bodies that might fall into a river.

Peru's ocean coast is home to tiny anchovies, which are caught for food and also feed larger saltwater fish, such as tuna. Other large fish off the coast include mackerel, swordfish, and bass, which are caught and sold for food. Sea mammals found in Peru include humpback whales, which spend some time off the northern coast, dolphins, and sea turtles. The Ballestas Islands, south of Lima, are known for their sea lions and seals.

The Ballestas Islands off the coast of central Peru abound with wildlife. Sea lions play in the water, and millions of birds nest on the rocky islands.

In the Skies

As with other kinds of wildlife, Peru has a great diversity of birds. Experts say more than 1,800 species live there. Along the coast, the birds include cormorants and Peruvian boobies. Both of these types of birds leave large amounts of their waste on Peru's small islands and coastal cliffs. Dried in the sun, the waste is called guano, and it is great fertilizer for crops. Collecting and selling the guano was once a major industry in Peru.

Birds found off the coast include hummingbirds, macaws, parrots, and condors. One of the world's largest flying birds, the Andean condor can weigh more than 30 pounds (14 kg) and have a wingspan of more than 10 feet (3 m). Even with wings that long, the birds need to ride air currents found over canyons and other windy areas to stay in flight.

National Bird: Cock-of-the-Rock

The Andean cock-of-the-rock lives in cloud forests. These forests are found on mountainsides above the rain forests, and are often covered with clouds or fog. Cock-of-the-rocks are found at elevations up to about 9,000 feet (2,700 m). The males are colorful, with bright red or orange feathers that cover the upper half of their bodies and fall over their beaks. They use their colorful markings and a call that has been compared to a squealing pig to attract females. The females are mostly brown, which helps them blend into the cliffs where they usually build their nests.

National Tree: Cinchona

The cinchona is a tree found on slopes across the Andes. It is Peru's national tree. It can grow to a height of about 30 feet (9 m). The Incas made a powder from its bark that they used to treat the disease malaria. During the 1800s, scientists learned that a chemical in the bark, called quinine, fought the disease. Peruvians have also used the bark to increase appetite and treat certain stomach problems. In 2008, the Peruvian government planted thousands of the trees, in part to promote scientific study of them.

Much smaller fliers in Peru are insects and butterflies. Peru is home to nearly four thousand species of butterflies. One of them is the owl butterfly. It has large circles on its wings that

Butterflies fly slowly, so they are an easy target for birds and other predators. When the owl butterfly lands, however, its large "eye" often scares off predators.

National Flower: Cantuta

The cantuta is a shrub that grows in the Andes and can reach a height of 10 feet (3 m). It produces a long, trumpet-shaped flower that attracts hummingbirds, and is the national flower of Peru. The flower is sometimes called the sacred flower of the Incas and probably played a role in some religious ceremonies. Some native people still use the flower during burials.

look like an owl's eyes. This helps keep away animals that might want to eat it.

The top of the trees in the rain forest is called the canopy. Some parks have built hanging walkways through the canopy so visitors can view the treetops and the abundant wildlife that lives there.

Plant Life

Peru has tens of thousands of types of plants, including several thousand different kinds of orchids that grow in the rain forest. The country is also known for its totora reeds, which grow in swampy areas and are used to make boats and Lake Titicaca's man-made floating islands. A grass found in that region and across the altiplano is ichu, which is used to feed some animals. The Incas and other native people before them used hundreds of plants as part of religious ceremonies meant to heal illnesses or improve health.

Today, one of the most controversial of these traditional plants is coca. People of the Andes chew the leaves for a boost of energy or to numb some pains. The leaves are also the source of the dangerous illegal drug cocaine. Peru has tried to convince farmers to grow other crops rather than coca plants.

A plant found only in the Andes and that catches the eye of many people who visit Peru is the *Puya raimondii*, the world's tallest flowering plant. It's also called the Queen of the Andes and can reach a height of more than 30 feet (9 m). A *Puya raimondii* can live for a hundred years or more before it begins to flower. After it flowers, it dies.

The spectacular *Puya raimondii* lives high in the Andes, at about 13,000 feet (4,000 m).

CHAPTER 4

Empires and Independence

THE FIRST SETTLERS OF WHAT BECAME PERU CAME from Asia and reached the region more than thirteen thousand years ago. Scientists have found remains of a fishing village along the northern coast dating to about that time, and in 2014 they announced they had found a settlement in the Andes almost as old. At 14,300 feet (4,400 m) above sea level, the site is the world's highest known settlement from that period. Items left behind by the people who lived in both these regions showed that they fished and hunted vicuña, among other animals, to survive.

Over the centuries, people spread out across Peru, going down the coast and reaching the Amazon rain forest and the area around Lake Titicaca. The early people were nomads, meaning they moved from place to place to hunt for food

Opposite: **The Moche culture flourished about two thousand years ago. The Moche people made the most realistic sculpture of any pre-Hispanic people in the region.**

Uncovering the Past

More than any Peruvian before him, Julio C. Tello (1880-1947) led the efforts to learn more about Peru's ancient cultures. Born in the Andean highlands, he was a native speaker of Quechua. He went to college, which was rare for indigenous people of the time, and received a degree in medicine. Tello then convinced the Peruvian government to send him to schools in the United States and Europe so he could train in archaeology—the study of ancient peoples through the buildings and artifacts they left behind. Tello's work in Peru included exploring Wari and Chavín sites. He also discovered four hundred mummies that came from the Paracas culture. Tello worked to make sure items he and others uncovered would be preserved. He has been called the father of archaeology in Peru.

and gather wild plants and seeds. But about nine thousand years ago, some people settled in permanent communities and began raising crops. Some of the earliest crops were peanuts, squash, and cotton, followed by beans, tomatoes, and corn. The people also domesticated llamas, alpacas, and guinea pigs, which were raised for their meat.

The Rise of Great Cultures

With the coming of settled communities and agriculture, some Peruvians began to build more complex societies, with some people serving as religious leaders and others as political leaders. One of the first great Peruvian cultures was the Chavín, which developed in the central Andes about three thousand years ago. They left behind art and the remains of buildings. Their culture, along with some of the items they made, such as ceramic pots and cloth, spread throughout large parts of Peru.

Other important cultures that followed the Chavín were the Paracas in the south and the Nazca along the coast. The Paracas were famous for their textiles, while the Nazca left behind huge lines carved into the desert. They pushed aside dark stones on the surface, letting the lighter soil underneath

The Nazca people made huge drawings of creatures in Peru's southern desert. This monkey is 310 feet (95 m) long, about the length of a football field.

appear. Seen from above, the lines form shapes and the outlines of animals. Scientists are not sure how the Nazca made the lines so precise.

Around the same time of the Nazca, about two thousand years ago, the Moche culture developed in the north. They left behind clay pots in the shapes of animals, plants, and people.

An important group of people in the south-central Peruvian Andes, near what is now Ayacucho, was the Wari. Around 600 CE, they created a small empire, controlling lands far from their central city. The Wari built roads to link these regions.

The Great Inca Empire

While the Wari and others created important cultures, one group came to dominate all of Peru: the Incas. They were based in Cusco, and by the end of the 1200s they were spread-

The City of Chan Chan

Starting around 1000 CE, the Chimú culture developed and grew around what is now Trujillo. Around 1300, the Chimú built Chan Chan, the largest city in all the Americas before the arrival of the Spanish. At its peak, about fifty thousand people lived there, in buildings made of dried mud and straw bricks, called adobe. This building material is often used in desert areas. Chan Chan was the largest adobe city ever built, with about ten thousand buildings. Some walls were 30 feet (9 m) tall. Since the time of the Chimú, however, much of the adobe has crumbled. Scientists have restored one part of the city, which tourists can visit today.

ing their influence through the nearby valley. The Incas spoke Quechua. In that language, *Inca* means "king." Sometimes they gained lands by marrying into the ruling families of other peoples. Other times they defeated people in war. And still other times, just the threat of war would lead another group to surrender to Inca rule. The Incas believed that their gods had given them the right to rule others.

The Incas took goods from the defeated peoples and then forced them to perform work for them. Through this work, the Incan rulers built palaces, government buildings, and more. Linking the parts of the empire was a huge road system, with two main highways running north and south. By the time the Spanish arrived, the Incas had built 25,000 miles (40,000 km) of roads.

During the 1400s, the Incan rulers extended their empire beyond modern-day Peru into parts of what are now Ecuador, Bolivia, Chile, Argentina, and Colombia. They called their empire Tawantinsuyu. The name means "four parts together," because the Incas divided their land into four sections. During the late

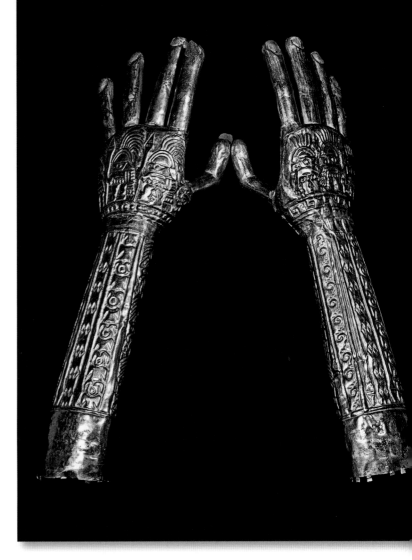

Many Peruvian cultures made exquisite gold objects. The Chimú made these golden burial gloves, which were discovered in a tomb.

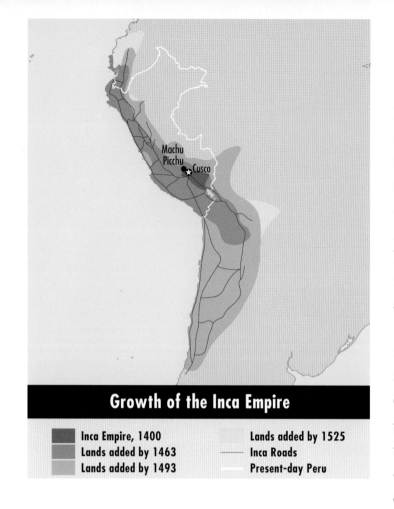

Growth of the Inca Empire

- Inca Empire, 1400
- Lands added by 1463
- Lands added by 1493
- Lands added by 1525
- — Inca Roads
- — Present-day Peru

1520s, however, the empire faced a crisis, as King Wayna Qhapaq's sons Atahualpa and Waskar battled each other to control the empire after his death. In 1532, Atahualpa defeated Waskar, but he soon faced a bigger problem: the arrival of the Spanish conquistadores, or conquerors.

Spanish Conquest and Rule

Starting in 1492, Italian explorer Christopher Columbus made four voyages to the Americas for Spain. He was followed by other explorers and conquistadores—soldiers seeking to claim lands for Spain in the region. Spain wanted to take the natural resources found in the Americas, particularly gold and silver. Spanish kings also wanted to spread their religion, Roman Catholicism, among the indigenous people they conquered.

In 1532, Francisco Pizarro reached the coast of Peru and then moved into the interior. Several years before, he had traveled along the coast of South America and learned of the great wealth the Incas had. When he returned, he was determined to seize those riches. After exchanging messages and gifts with the Incan king, Pizarro and his roughly 180 soldiers met Atahualpa and his much larger army in the town of Cajamarca. Although

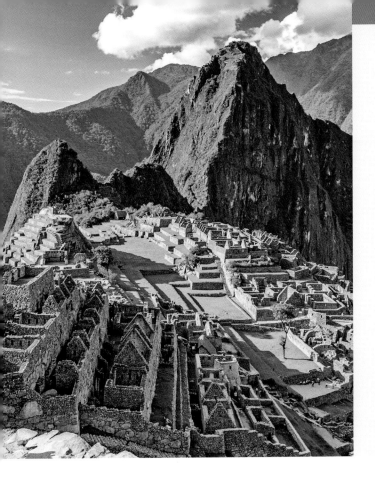

A Tour of Machu Picchu

The Incan kings built many grand homes for themselves, but the best known today is at Machu Picchu. Most people outside of Peru did not know about this royal city at 7,972 feet (2,430 m) in the Andes until the twentieth century. Now, it is Peru's most popular destination for tourists. Machu Picchu was built during the 1400s by Pachacuti, an Incan king who greatly expanded the empire. It features a large plaza that separated the site's religious temples and royal buildings from the area where common people lived and worked. Some of the workers raised crops on flat land, called terraces, cut into mountainsides. The Incas raised food this way throughout the empire. The Incas constructed the buildings at Machu Picchu by arranging huge stones together so tightly that they didn't need any kind of sticky substance to join them. The Incas are still admired today for their building skills.

badly outnumbered, Pizarro and his men had better weapons and stronger armor. They also had horses, which amazed the Incas, since there were no horses in South America at the time. Using a surprise attack, Pizarro and his men captured Atahualpa and killed him. Pizarro and his men then went to Cusco to take control of the government.

Soon the Spanish set up a new capital city in Lima. They let an Incan king loyal to them rule, but the Spanish were the actual leaders of the colony they called Peru. Some Incan royalty rebelled, but they were never able to defeat the better-equipped conquistadores. Many people also died from diseases the Spanish brought with them from Europe, including smallpox.

From Lima, ships began to carry gold and silver back to Spain. Meanwhile, the Spanish set up a system they used in other colonies, the *encomienda*. Under this system, Spanish colonists claimed land and received any crops or goods that the local native people produced on it. Over time, the Spaniards demanded more from the encomienda workers. If the workers could not produce it, they were forced to sell the land to the Spaniards. Other indigenous people worked as servants. As part of the encomienda system, the Spaniards also forced the local peoples to construct buildings, make clothing, and work in the

In 1532, Francisco Pizarro and his men captured the Inca king Atahualpa, who was killed the following year. Pizarro himself was killed in 1541 by other Spaniards in a dispute over who controlled the wealthy Incan capital of Cusco.

The Last King

After the Spanish conquest, several Incan kings tried to keep an independent state in Peru. The last of them was Túpac Amaru (ca. 1540–1572). His father, Manco Inca, was a brother of Atahualpa and had briefly led an army against the Spanish. Manco Inca set up his own government in Vilcabamba, located in forests west of Cusco. Túpac Amaru grew up learning the traditional Incan religious beliefs. He resisted Spanish rule and the Catholic teachings they brought. When Túpac Amaru's ruling brother died in 1571, Túpac Amaru became the king of the Incan state in Vilcabamba. He didn't rule long, however, as Spanish forces came to the city the next year to wipe out the Incan government there. Túpac Amaru fled the city before they arrived, carrying a religious image of the sun and mummies of some of his dead relatives. The Spanish, though, caught up with Túpac Amaru, took him to Cusco, and cut off his head. His last words, translated into English, were said to be, "Mother Earth, witness how my enemies spill my blood."

gold and silver mines. They also raised crops and animals that the settlers brought from Europe, such as wheat and cattle.

After the last of the Incan rebellions, many of the people began to accept Spanish rule. Spain won the support of some local leaders by giving them land and a role to play in governing the large number of common Incas. But they disrupted life for many other Incan peoples by forcing them into new villages. This effort was meant to make it easier to convert the local people to Christianity and work for the colonists. Spain's major concern was getting as much wealth as it could from Peru.

The caption inside the image reads:
ac, y Dª Beatris Cuziquiuay; Que el à de 1558 Rezi vieron el Sⁿ Sacramento del Baut...ⁿ Siendo | Arzo obispo qᵉ fue d Toledo, y Dⁿ Franⁿ henrriq Cuya Dama dela Reyna ñra Sª, f Caso en el Marqˢ d Feria Alma el Reý, Dⁿ primer Monarca del Peru fue ela, de Hoo fundo la gran Ciud del Cuzco Cabeza, desteᵏ Impⁿ d ste Maᵗ d Aleᵗ Caso con Dⁿ Ana dla Cueba henrrᶻ hija y herm de los Duqˢ d Alborrucrqˢ y del Cõd d Caˢtelar Vir q fue d el Peruᵏ Yhi Dⁿia Ana Maria Coya de Loyoh y lalle zaron a Eſpaña, y su Maᵗ en atencion i a la R, Sangreqˢ le asis hono, y Dⁿ Henrrin hermᵗ d la Cueba Incad l aronl a Dⁿ Ysabel, y a Dⁿ Ana henrrii d la Cueba Cuzc d el... a Sⁿ ...I P I.

From Colony to Independence

European diseases and the forced resettlement of people led to the death of several million native Peruvians. Needing more workers, the Spanish brought in slaves from Africa. Some enslaved Africans worked at mines or raised crops such as sugar and coffee, while others worked in cities. By 1636, enslaved Africans made up one-third of the population in Lima. By the end of that century Lima was the largest city in South America. It was the seat of a government called the viceroyalty. Spanish officials in Lima controlled the affairs of Spain's colonies across much of South America.

Society in colonial Peru was divided into distinct classes.

At the top were the officials sent from Spain. Below them were the *criollos*, people with Spanish roots who had been born in Peru, and mestizos, people with both Spanish and Indian roots. Further below were free blacks and people of mixed African and Spanish or native descent. At the bottom were native peoples and African slaves. In the 1700s,

A cup made in Peru in about 1650 shows an Inca leader, a European trumpet player, and an African drummer. It is one of the earliest pieces of indigenous art that depicts an African in South America.

Rubber trees produce a milky juice called latex, which is used to make rubber. To extract the latex, slits are made in the bark, allowing the latex to run into cups that are attached to the tree.

began to produce rubber. They did the hard farm work, while the wealthy made money from selling the rubber. Their condition did not improve in the early years of the twentieth century, though the government did build more hospitals and schools across the country.

The country continued to be led by strongmen, leaders who ruled by force like the earlier caudillos. They favored the wealthy who lived along the coast, and did not promote genuine democracy. For example, during the 1920s the government outlawed a party that wanted to weaken foreign influence and promote the interests of indigenous peoples.

Peru and the rest of the world entered a difficult time in 1929. That marked the start of the Great Depression, a severe economic downturn. Companies had to lay off many workers. Other countries no longer had money to buy Peruvian rubber or other resources. At the end of the 1930s, World War II (1939–1945) began. The war stretched around the globe, as the Allies, led by the United Kingdom, the United States,

Russia, and France, battled the Axis powers of Germany, Japan, and Italy. Peru did not formally join the war, but it worked with the Allies, allowing them to use its ports and airfields and selling them valuable resources such as oil and cotton.

In the early twentieth century, Peru's leaders typically worked for the interests of the wealthy. In 1924, Víctor Raúl Haya de la Torre (above the crowd) formed the American Popular Revolutionary Alliance, which tried to enact reforms on behalf of workers and indigenous people.

Japanese-Peruvians during World War II

Japanese immigrants began coming to Peru during the end of the nineteenth century. By the time Japan attacked the U.S. naval base at Pearl Harbor, Hawaii, in 1941, Peru was home to about twenty-five thousand people of Japanese descent. Many had been born in Peru and spoke only Spanish, not Japanese. Nevertheless, because of anti-Japanese sentiment, the United States asked Peru and other South American nations to arrest some of their Japanese residents, and about 2,200 Japanese-Peruvians were sent to prison camps in the United States. Many of the 2,200 were later sent to Japan, and some remained in the United States after the war ended. Only a few Japanese-Peruvians ever returned to Peru.

Peru continued to experience cruel and authoritarian governments until the 1950s, when it held free elections. Many native peoples began to move from the mountains to the coastal cities, a process that continues today. That movement helped make Lima one of the largest cities in the Americas. During the 1960s, the increased openness in elections and governments chipped away at some of the power of the wealthy, though not all. In 1968, the military returned to power, and although it limited free speech and political freedoms, it also tried to help some of Peru's poor. Under General Juan Velasco, the government took over some foreign-owned properties. It also took land from some rich Peruvians and gave it to the poor. Velasco made Quechua, the language of the Incas, an official language of the country.

New Conflicts, New Hopes

Members of the military forced Velasco from power in 1975. The generals who ruled agreed to free elections in 1980, but Peru still faced great inequality and many people demanded more rights. During the 1980s, two revolutionary groups emerged—Sendero Luminoso ("Shining Path") and the Túpac Amaru Revolutionary Movement. Peru entered an era of bloodshed, as the rebels fought with the government and killed people who refused to support them. The Shining Path was a particularly violent group, and the government's efforts to stop them led to almost seventy thousand deaths. Many of the dead were innocent Peruvians, mostly indigenous people, caught up in the conflict and killed by the Peruvian military.

In the mid-twentieth century, many people began moving to Lima from other parts of the country. There was not enough housing, so they built makeshift houses on the outskirts of the city. Even today, many of these neighborhoods lack running water.

Doing Things for Themselves

As the Shining Path spread terror through the Andes, the people of Ayacucho and other areas formed *rondas campesinas*—peasant patrols. Seeing that the national government could not do much to battle the rebels in remote areas, the rondas campesinas resisted the Shining Path with violence. Later, the Peruvian military helped create more of these groups, which were also called self-defense committees. Even before the rise of the Shining Path, some rural Peruvians in the north had formed rondas campesinas to battle crime. They also helped settle local disputes and build public buildings. Some villages relied on the work of the rondas campesinas into the 2000s.

Some of the rebels' activities were paid for by the growing and selling of coca, which was used to make cocaine. The Shining Path, for example placed a "tax" on coca paste produced in remote areas it controlled. The United States sent military aid to help Peru fight the groups who supported the drug trade. But poor farmers continued to grow coca because they could make more money from it than from other crops.

The violence in Peru and economic troubles led some to call the 1980s the country's "Lost Decade." Starting in 1990, President Alberto Fujimori tried to both end the violence and improve the economy. His record was mixed, though. The violence ended, but many indigenous people still struggled to earn a good living. And Fujimori's government used bribes and other illegal measures to stay in power. He was forced to leave Peru in 2000 and was eventually brought back to serve time in prison.

In the twenty-first century, Peru has seen some improvements. Prices for its natural resources have been mostly strong. But the gap between the wealthy and the large number of poor people remains large. Peru faces challenges, but its people will face them directly, as they have in the past.

President Alberto Fujimori speaks to the public two weeks after he declared a state of emergency and shut down Congress in April 1992. He had grown frustrated with the Congress's lack of support for his policies, so he carried out what has been called a presidential coup. The following year, under the new constitution, his supporters won a majority of the seats in Congress.

CHAPTER 5

Serving the People

AFTER HUNDREDS OF YEARS OF BEING LED BY men sent from Spain, Peru has been independent for almost two hundred years. Peruvians have elected many of their own leaders, but at times, military leaders have seized power, and the people could not freely vote for whom they chose. Today, Peru is a strong democracy, with regular elections that let the people choose their leaders at all levels of government. All citizens eighteen years and older are required to vote. They can be fined if they don't have a good reason for not voting.

Like other democratic countries, the form of Peru's government and its basic laws are outlined in its constitution. Peru has had several constitutions since it gained independence. The most recent one was created in 1993, though it has been amended, or changed, several times since then. The constitution calls for three distinct branches of government at the national level: executive, legislative, and judicial.

Opposite: **Every day, an elaborate changing of the guard ceremony is held outside the Government Palace, the site of the president's offices.**

Pedro Pablo Kuczynski is the son of a Christian mother and Jewish father. He was born in Lima in 1936, two years after his parents had fled Nazi persecution in Germany. Growing up, Kuczynski watched his father, a doctor, treat some of Peru's poorest people, and he decided he would one day work to help those Peruvians. He studied in both Great Britain and the United States before working for an international agency and holding several government positions in Peru. Known to Peruvians as P.P.K., Kuczynski ran for president in 2016. He did not do well in the first election but managed to win enough votes to force a runoff with Keiko Fujimori, the daughter of former president Alberto Fujimori. Kuczynski won that election by just thirty-nine thousand votes, out of a total of eighteen million. He pledged to improve education and medical care and create more jobs.

The Executive Branch

Peru's executive branch of government is led by the country's president. The president's main duty is to carry out the country's laws. A candidate for president must be at least thirty-five years old, been born in Peru, and have the legal right to vote. During an election, if no candidate receives more than half of the vote, the two candidates with the most votes face each other in a special election. Once elected, a president serves for five years and can run again, but not in the election immediately following the first term of office.

The president's first duty is to enforce the constitution and the laws passed by Congress. The president also manages

A Visit to the Capital

The Spanish set up their capital in Lima in 1535, preferring the coastal climate there to the colder weather in Cusco in the Andes. Lima also offered a port that Spanish ships could use. An earthquake in 1746 destroyed most of the city, but the Spanish quickly rebuilt it. The city was badly damaged again during the War of the Pacific, when Chilean troops controlled Lima. Today, Lima has a population of nearly eight million people, making it one of the largest cities in the Americas.

Located in Peru's coastal desert, Lima is the second-driest capital city in the world. Moisture, when it comes, usually is a misty fog called *garúa*. Much of the population growth in recent years has come from

indigenous people leaving the countryside to find work in the capital.

Lima is the economic engine of Peru. It is the heart of the nation's financial industry, has thousands of factories, and contains one of the largest ports in South America. It is also the nation's education center. The National University of San Marcos was founded in 1551, making it the oldest continuously operating university in the Americas.

The historic central part of the city includes the Plaza de Armas, which features a bronze fountain that dates to 1650. Along the plaza is the Presidential Palace, where tourists can see the daily changing of the palace guard. The city's main cathedral is nearby. Because of earthquakes, it has been rebuilt several times since the sixteenth century.

The city is divided into many distinct neighborhoods. San Isidro has many offices for banks. It also contains an adobe pyramid at least 1,500 years old. Along the coast is Miraflores, which has cliffs that overlook the ocean. Nearby is Barranco, which, like Miraflores, is known for its nightlife. One of the city's best museums is located west of the central city. The Larco Museum has a huge collection of pottery, textiles, and other items dating back five thousand years.

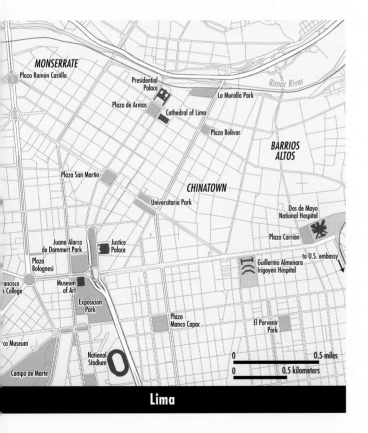

Lima

the country's defense, handles affairs with foreign nations, and preserves order within the country. Peru's president can propose laws to Congress and make comments on laws passed

The Flag of Peru

General José de San Martín chose the colors red and white for the Peruvian flag. Legend says he chose those colors because he saw flamingos flying when he first entered Peru. The red of the two outer vertical bands is said to stand for the blood shed during the war for independence, and the white of the middle vertical band stands for peace. In the center of the white stripe is a shield surrounded by palm and laurel leaves. The shield shows Peru's national animal, the vicuña; the national tree, the cinchona; and gold and silver coins pouring out of a horn called a cornucopia. The coins represent the wealth Peru gets from its natural resources. The Peruvian government made this its official flag in 1825. Today, most flags flown in Peru only have the red

and white bands. The shield appears only on flags used by the government.

by the legislature. But unlike in many countries, the president cannot prevent a law from taking effect.

Peru's executive branch includes two vice presidents. The first vice president becomes president if the elected president can't serve. If the first vice president can't serve, then the second vice president becomes president.

The executive branch also includes the president's advisers, known as the cabinet. The members of the cabinet lead the various departments of the executive branch, such as

President Pedro Pablo Kuczynski (center) attends a ceremony with military leaders and the minister of defense. The president is the supreme commander of Peru's armed forces.

agriculture, education, and defense. The cabinet has its own president, who is chosen by the nation's president. The cabinet president helps Peru's president choose the other members of the cabinet. The cabinet also approves proposed laws submitted to Congress by the president. When Congress grants the president power to make laws, the cabinet must approve them before they take effect.

The Peruvian Congress meets in a building called the Legislative Palace. The Congress began meeting there in 1912.

Making the Country's Laws

The legislative branch in Peru is called the Congress and it proposes and passes laws for the nation. Unlike the United

States and many other democracies, Peru's legislature has only one house, with 130 members. The members are elected for five-year terms. Anyone twenty-five years or older can run for Congress, as long as they were born in Peru and have the legal right to vote. Members of Congress choose a leader, called a president, who oversees activities when members meet to discuss possible laws.

Congress also selects some of it members to form the Permanent Assembly. Its duties include approving the selection of certain government officials who handle the country's financial matters.

A Peruvian woman drops her ballot in a box during an election. More than 80 percent of Peruvians vote in every election, a much higher percentage than in the United States.

Peru's Court System

The third branch of the government is the judicial. This consists of Peru's different courts. The most powerful court is the Supreme Court of Justice. It has sixteen members, including the chief justice, who is the head of the judicial branch. The Supreme Court reviews rulings made by lower courts. A separate court, the Tribunal of Constitutional Guarantees, decides if a law violates the country's constitution. Below these two courts are superior courts. The superior courts hear appeals of cases that come from lower courts.

Some judges and officials at the local level known as justices of the peace are elected by voters. Other judges are named by the president after receiving recommendations from the National Justice Council. Congress must approve the president's choices.

Peru's National Government

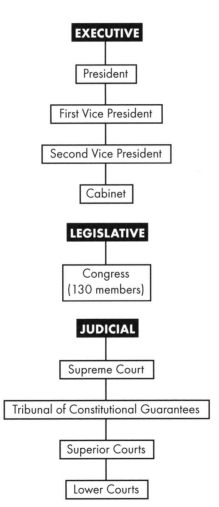

EXECUTIVE

President

First Vice President

Second Vice President

Cabinet

LEGISLATIVE

Congress
(130 members)

JUDICIAL

Supreme Court

Tribunal of Constitutional Guarantees

Superior Courts

Lower Courts

A teacher works with a student in Lima. In Peru, classes are typically small, with fewer than twenty students.

Local Government

Peru is divided into twenty-five regions. Lima does not belong to a region. Each elects a regional president, who serves a four-year term and leads the region's executive branch. The regions also elect legislators who form councils.

The regions are divided into smaller units called provinces. Peruvians elect mayors to run the executive branches of the country's 196 provinces. Within the provinces are about 1,600 cities and towns, known as municipalities. Residents in the provinces and municipalities also elect mayors and councillors. The different levels of regional and local government also have coordination councils, which are made up of both elected officials and citizens representing different groups in the area. These councils advise the regional presidents and mayors. The local governments receive money from the national government to pay for such things as roads and schools.

Peru's National Anthem

In 1821, General José de San Martín held a contest to create a national anthem for Peru. The winning song had words written by José de la Torre Ugarte and music by José Bernardo Alcedo. The song is known as both the "Himno Nacional del Perú" ("National Anthem of Peru") and the "Marcha Nacional" ("National March"). The original version is much longer than the one Peruvians commonly sing today.

Spanish lyrics

Somos libres, seámoslo siempre, seámoslo siempre,
Y antes niegue sus luces el sol,
Que faltemos al voto solemne
Que la Patria al Eterno elevó.
Que faltemos al voto solemne
Que la Patria al Eterno elevó.

Largo tiempo el peruano oprimido
la ominosa cadena arrastró,
Condenado a cruel servidumbre
largo tiempo en silencio gimió.
Mas apenas el grito sagrado
¡Libertad! en sus costas se oyó
La indolencia de esclavo sacude,
la humillada cerviz levantó.

English translation

We are free; let us always be so,
And let the sun rather deny its light
Than that we should fail the solemn vow
Which our country raised to God.
Than that we should fail the solemn vow
Which our country raised to God.

For a long time the Peruvian, oppressed,
Dragged the ominous chain;
Condemned to cruel serfdom,
For a long time he moaned in silence.
But as soon as the sacred cry of
Freedom! was heard on his coasts,
He shook off the indolence of the slave,
He raised his humiliated head.

CHAPTER 6

Peru at Work

N INCAN TIMES, THE WEALTHIEST PERUVIANS WORE fine jewelry made of gold. Under Spanish rule, miners unearthed silver that was sent back to Spain. The mining of valuable metals such as these remains a large part of Peru's economy. While prices for these materials go up and down, on the whole they have been strong during the twenty-first century. That has helped Peru's economy grow faster than the economy in other parts of the region. In turn, the growth has helped several million Peruvians escape poverty. Still, in many remote areas, people struggle to find jobs that pay good wages. Improving the education system is key to helping more people find good jobs.

Opposite: **Many farmers in Peru use animals such as donkeys and cattle to work their fields.**

Peru is one of the world's leading fishing nations. More fish are caught in Peru than in any other nation in South America.

What Peru Grows, Makes, and Mines

AGRICULTURE (2014)
Sugarcane	11,300,000 metric tons
Potatoes	4,704,000 metric tons
Rice	2,896,000 metric tons

MANUFACTURING (2013)
Cement	10,526,000 metric tons
Textiles	32,311,000 meters
Steel ball bearings	182,100 metric tons

MINING (2014)
Iron	7,192,000 metric tons
Copper	1,379,000 metric tons
Zinc	1,318,000 metric tons

Farming and Fishing

The ancient people of Peru domesticated many crops, and some of them remain an important part of the economy. These include potatoes, quinoa, and cotton. In recent decades, Peru has built dams and improved irrigation, making more land available for farming, and agriculture has increased. That process continues today. Agriculture accounts for about 7 percent of the country's gross domestic product (GDP), the total of all the goods and services a country produces. About 19 percent of Peru's land is used for farming; most of this is used for grazing animals such as cattle, sheep, and goats. Along with their traditional crops, Peruvian farmers grow vegetables such as artichoke and asparagus to sell abroad. In 2014, Peru exported more asparagus than any other country. Blueberries, grapes, and coffee are also exported.

Thanks to the Peru Current, fishing off the coast of the country is excellent. Anchovies are one important catch. The tiny fish are turned into oil and fish meal, which is used to

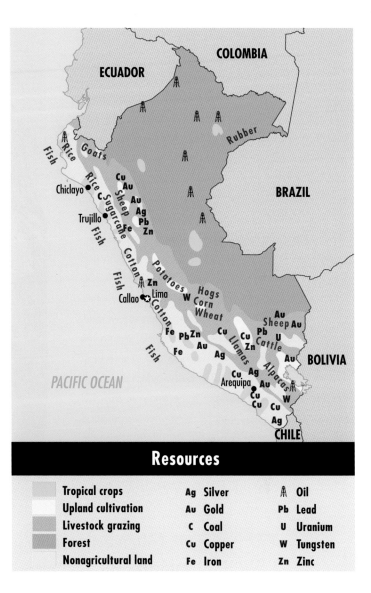

Resources

Tropical crops		Ag	Silver	⚒	Oil
Upland cultivation		Au	Gold	Pb	Lead
Livestock grazing		C	Coal	U	Uranium
Forest		Cu	Copper	W	Tungsten
Nonagricultural land		Fe	Iron	Zn	Zinc

Growing the Super Grain

Quinoa has sometimes been called a super grain, because of the amount of protein it contains. Technically, though, it is not a grain but rather a relative of spinach. It also doesn't contain gluten, a substance found in wheat and many other grains that can make some people sick. Peruvians have been growing quinoa in the Andes for thousands of years, but in recent decades, people around the world have started eating it. That has been good news for Peruvian quinoa growers. Quinoa can be grown at sea level or as high as 12,000 feet (3,700 m) and it needs little water compared to many other crops. Almost half of Peru's quinoa farmers are women. For a time, the rising popularity of quinoa around the world led to a sharp increase in its cost. Some food experts worried that the rising cost would make it too expensive for poor Peruvians in the Andes to buy. But a study in 2016 found that the rising price was a good thing overall. Poor people could still afford it, and the growers benefited by making more money.

feed fish raised on fish farms. Fishers also catch mackerel and sardines. The fish caught off Peru and the products made from them are also important exports for the country.

Riches from the Earth

Mining is a key part of the Peruvian economy, and the materials mined are its top export. Peru ranks third in the world in the amount of copper it produces, and vast amounts of copper remain beneath the ground. The country is also among the world leaders in mining silver, gold, zinc, iron, and tin. In

Weights and Measures

Peruvians use the metric system to weigh and measure most items. One exception, however, is gasoline, which is measured in gallons.

2015, about two hundred thousand Peruvians worked in the mining industry. Many mines in Peru are owned by companies based overseas. For all sectors of the economy, China is Peru's top trading partner, followed by the United States.

Some of the country's iron is used to make steel, and other minerals are processed in the country before they are shipped overseas. The processing involves taking the metal out of the rock around it and preparing it for use in finished goods. Zinc is one of the metals commonly processed in the country.

Other products from the ground include petroleum and natural gas. Much of these are found in the Amazon.

Peruvian gold miners work underground high in the Andes. Peru is the second-largest gold producer in the Western Hemisphere, trailing only the United States.

Money Facts

The main unit of currency in Peru is the nuevo sol, which is often called just the sol. One sol is divided into 100 céntimos. Peru has coins worth 1, 2, and 5 soles, and bills worth 10, 20, 50, 100, and 200 soles. There are also coins worth 1, 5, 10, 20, and 50 céntimos. The government issued new paper currency in 2011, but old bills are still accepted. The fronts of the bills show the face of important people in Peruvian history. For example, the 50-sol bill shows Abraham Valdelomar Pinto (1888–1919), a writer and illustrator. In 2017, 1 sol equaled US$0.31, and US$1.00 equaled 3.25 soles.

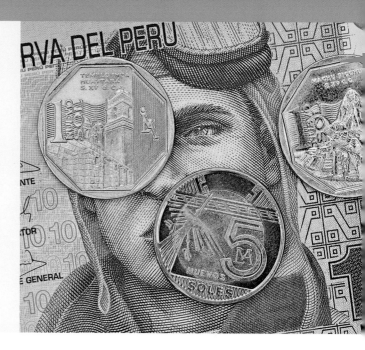

Making Goods

Industry, including mining and making products out of petroleum, or oil, makes up about 34 percent of the GDP. Some of Peru's key manufactured goods are cement, textiles, chemical products, equipment for mining and construction, and food sold in stores.

Chocolate from the Amazon

Along with its other crops, Peru produces cacao beans, the source for chocolate. Cacao is grown in the Amazon, and that is where Elizabeth Gómez Flores launched Nativos in 2011. Her company sells Amazon chocolate that is grown without chemicals. She mixes the chocolate with other ingredients grown in the region, including herbs, coffee, pineapple, and mango. Flores started her company in her home but soon expanded to her own small factory. Her chocolates are sold across Peru and are available through the internet.

To help sell goods overseas, Peru promotes free trade with other nations. This means Peru and its international partners put few limits on what they buy and sell from each other. Peru has trade agreements with the United States, Japan, Canada, China, and many other nations.

Providing Services

The service sector makes up the largest part of Peru's economy, accounting for about 58 percent of the GDP. The service

A worker monitors a furnace at a foundry in Lima. Peru produces many metal products such as steel and iron.

economy includes such things as banking, education, health care, government, and the sale of goods at stores and restaurants. In Peru, financial services and telecommunications (phone and internet) make up a large part of this sector. Most telecommunications businesses are located along the more

A woman buys produce at a market in Urubamba. About three out of every five workers in Peru are employed in the service sector of the economy.

highly populated coast. Some remote parts of the Andes and Amazon lack phone and internet service. In 2014, just 40 percent of the entire population used the internet.

To grow the economy as a whole, Peru hopes to improve its transportation services. That means building more roads and improving airports. Lima is the center for international plane arrivals, and the country has several airlines that fly within the country. Air transportation is crucial for another part of the service economy: tourism. People come from around the world to visit Machu Picchu and other ancient sites or to explore the wildlife in the Peruvian Amazon. In 2014, about 2.6 million people from other countries visited Peru, and tourism was worth about $4 billion that year to the country's economy.

CHAPTER 7

The People of Peru

THE LAND THE INCAS CONQUERED WAS HOME TO different indigenous groups. The descendants of many of these people can still be found across the country, mostly in the highlands and the Amazon region. Spaniards first arrived in what is now Peru in the 1500s, and since then people of other racial and ethnic backgrounds have come to Peru, adding to its diversity.

Opposite: **Peruvians fill a pedestrian street in Lima. About one out of every three Peruvians lives in the capital city or its suburbs.**

Population of Major Cities (2017 est.)

Lima	7,737,002
Arequipa	841,130
Callao	813,264
Trujillo	747,450
Chiclayo	577,375

In recent years, newcomers have continued to arrive in Peru. Many come from neighboring Chile seeking work. Still, over the last decade, more than two million people have left Peru, hoping to find better jobs or attend schools in other countries. Many have gone to Argentina, Spain, and the United States.

Peru has seen a steady growth in its population in the twenty-first century, going from about twenty-six million in 2000 to more than thirty-two million in 2017. About four out of five Peruvians live in urban areas, most along the coast.

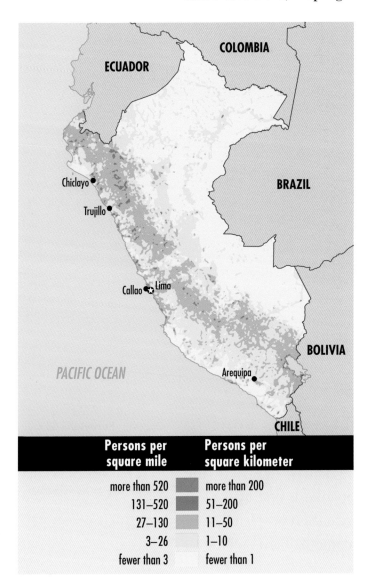

Persons per square mile	Persons per square kilometer
more than 520	more than 200
131–520	51–200
27–130	11–50
3–26	1–10
fewer than 3	fewer than 1

European and Asian Influence

Although greatly outnumbered by the Incas and other indigenous people, the Spanish conquered Peru and shaped its history. Today, white people of European descent make up only 15 percent of the population of Peru, but they and some mestizos still largely control the country's government and society.

Peruvian immigrants celebrate their homeland at a parade in New York City. More than four hundred thousand Peruvian immigrants live in the United States.

After Peru gained its independence, settlers from other parts of Europe came to the country, especially from France, Italy, Germany, and the United Kingdom. They sometimes formed their own distinct communities. For example, many German-speaking people settled in the Pasco region in central Peru. Oxapampa and Pozuzo, two towns there, have some buildings that look like ones found in the Alps of Austria, and some restaurants serve German food.

Peru's Racial and Ethnic Groups

Indigenous	45%
Mestizo	37%
White	15%
Black, Japanese, Chinese, and other	3%

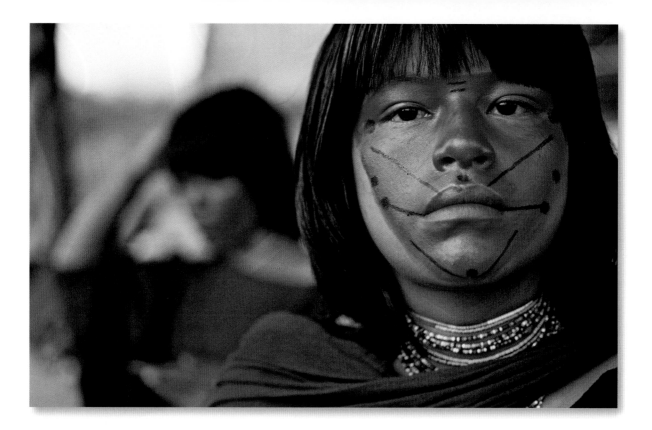

Asháninka people apply red face paint each day. They vary the design day to day, depending on their mood.

Indigenous Peoples

Indigenous people make up almost half of the population of Peru, and they belong to more than fifty different ethnic groups. The largest of these are the Quechua, Aymara, and Asháninka. Others include the Aguarana, Shipibo, and the Yagua. About 13 percent of the country speaks Quechua, one of the country's three official languages, along with Spanish and Aymara. In large cities, people who speak Quechua are likely to use the language at home and speak Spanish in public. Fewer Peruvians speak Aymara, Asháninka, and the more than forty other indigenous languages found in Peru. The country's constitution says some of these other languages can be considered official in regions where one particular language is most commonly used.

In recent years, some indigenous people from the Amazon have chosen to come out of the rain forest to make contact with tourists and scientists. In Peru, one of these groups is the Mashco Piro. In 2006, the Peruvian government began a policy

A teacher writes on a blackboard during a Spanish lesson at a school in a Quechua community. All indigenous children in Peru learn Spanish in school.

Remote tribes like the Mashco Piro are called *aislados*—Spanish for "isolated people." In recent years, some have left their traditional lands as logging and mining have spread in the Peruvian Amazon. The group Survival International keeps track of small groups of indigenous people around the world. In 2016, it predicted the aislados could eventually be wiped out as they lose traditional hunting lands and are exposed to new diseases. At times, these groups also fight with each other as they compete for resources. Peru has a government department that is supposed to help the Mashco Piro and other isolated groups. But it does not receive much money, and the companies that mine and cut trees in the forest have a lot of influence with the government. That influence lets them continue their work in the land of the aislados.

of not making contact with mostly hidden groups such as the Mashco Piro for fear that the indigenous people would contract common diseases for which their bodies had no immunity. But by 2015, the Mashco Piro were making more frequent contact with strangers, and officials are working to understand why, without forcing encounters with the Mashco Piro.

Afro-Peruvians

The descendants of African slaves brought to Peru make up a small part of the country's population today. About one hundred thousand enslaved Africans were brought to Peru until slavery was outlawed. Most worked on large farms called plantations, but others worked in Lima. In the city, they built many of the buildings, worked as household servants, and ran small businesses. Since first arriving in the Americas, Afro-Peruvians have made great contributions to the country's arts and culture. Some enslaved people managed to escape and set up small communities called *palenques*. One of these was in the region called Chincha, south of Lima, and the Afro-Peruvian presence is still strong there today.

Afro-Peruvians prepare to perform at a festival at La Quebrada, in the Chincha region.

CHAPTER 8

Spiritual Life

94

ACROSS PERU, ROMAN CATHOLIC CHURCHES built by the Spanish can be found in the center of many cities and towns. The Spanish tried to convert the Incas and other indigenous people to their religion. Most native people were forced to accept Christian teaching, blending their own traditional beliefs with the new faith that spread across their land. In remote areas today, some people still hold and practice some of the ideas and customs that existed before the Spanish arrived.

Opposite: **Incense fills the air during a Catholic procession in Lima.**

Evangelical Protestants take part in a worship service in Iquitos.

In recent decades, Peru has also seen a growing number of its people turn to Protestant faiths. Immigrants from Asia and the Middle East brought their religions with them to Peru, too. While today most Peruvians call themselves Catholic, the country allows everyone to worship as they please.

Ancient Beliefs

As the Incas conquered Peru, they encountered people with different religious beliefs. In general, the Incas let the conquered people keep their beliefs and practices or combine

Religion in Peru	
Roman Catholicism	81.3%
Evangelical Protestant	12.5%
Other	3.3%
None	2.9%

them with Incan beliefs. In one example, the Incas kept a temple devoted to Pachacamac, a god worshipped by some people who lived along the coast south of Peru. Nearby, the Incas built a temple to the sun, which they worshipped and called Inti. The major temple for Inti was in Cusco, but the Incas had hundreds of important religious sites throughout their empire. The Incas also worshipped the moon and many other things found in nature. They believed mountains had

Shamans make offerings during a ritual, thanking the earth for all it provides.

Visitors to the city of Arequipa can see the remains of a part of Incan religious life. Juanita is the name given to a young Incan girl who was left on Mount Ampato about five hundred years ago. Ice and snow preserved her body, which was discovered in 1995. Now, Juanita's mummified body is on display. She was one of several young mummies that have been discovered on Peruvian mountaintops. The children were killed as a sacrifice to the mountain gods. The Incas, like many ancient people, thought that offering precious materials or even human bodies was a way to thank the gods. They believed the sacrifices would ensure that the gods would continue to give them rain, good crops, and other benefits.

spirits, which they called *apus*, and that on the mountain peaks people had better contact with the gods.

The Incas considered both their living and dead kings to be gods. The bodies of the dead rulers were turned into mummies. The Incas also made mummies of some common people, and their surviving relatives worshipped them.

Some ancient beliefs survive today. Many indigenous Peruvians still trek up mountains as part of religious ceremonies. And they trust healers, known as shamans, to help them using a wide range of natural remedies. Consuming some plants is supposed to enable people to talk to the spirits of dead relatives. The shamans also say they can predict the future after consuming some of these natural medicines.

An Ancient Ceremony Survives

Each year in June, the Incas held a festival called Inti Raymi to honor the sun god. This event occurred around the time of the winter solstice—the shortest day of the year. Only men with ties to the royal family took part. Over several days, they danced and sacrificed many llamas. A version of Inti Raymi is still held today in Cusco. Thousands of people wearing traditional Incan clothing take part in the festival, which features music and dancing. The people march from downtown Cusco to the remains of an Incan fort. Peruvians began the modern Inti Raymi festival in 1944 as a way to honor their Incan roots.

Modern Beliefs

The Spanish conquistadores who defeated the Incans were quickly followed by priests who tried to spread their Roman Catholic faith to the people of Peru. These priests, called missionaries, destroyed many of the Incas' religious objects and

In many Peruvian cities, including Cusco (left), the cathedral is the largest building, towering above those around it.

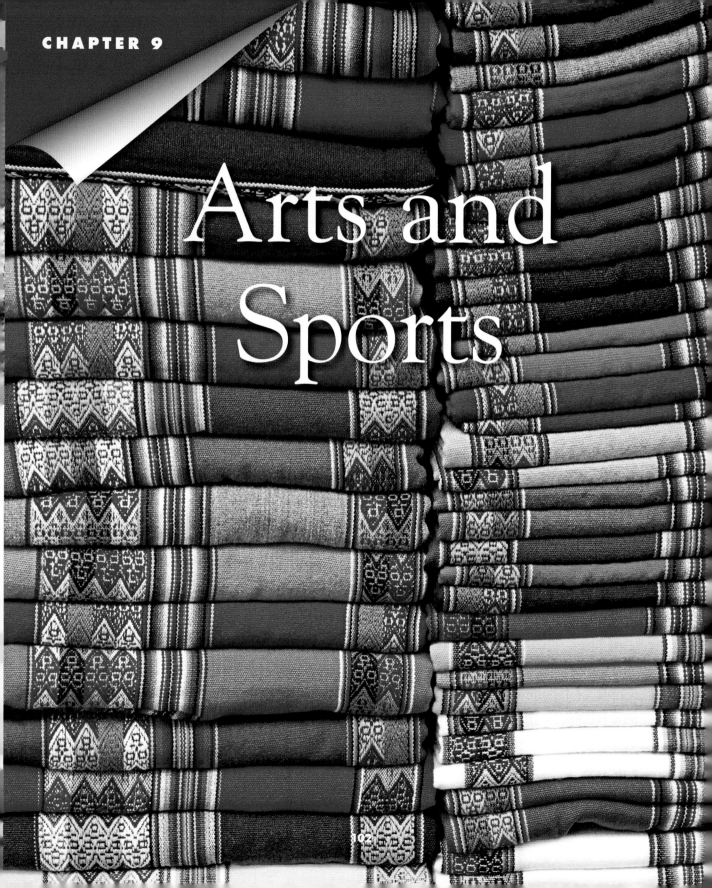

CHAPTER 9

Arts and Sports

LONG BEFORE THE INCAS ROSE TO POWER, THE different peoples of Peru made magnificent art. Some of it was practical, such as brightly colored textiles with geometric patterns. Some of it was gold items made for kings.

The Incas adopted some artistic styles that had already thrived in Peru for centuries. Then the Spanish brought different kinds of art and literature with them. Spanish art often focused on Christian themes. Other newcomers to Peru added to the country's artistic mix. Today, Peruvian artists produce

Opposite: **People in Peru have been making beautiful textiles since long before the Spanish arrived in South America.**

great works. Some reflect Peru's past, while others are focused on today's events and artistic trends practiced around the world. The different forms of art and popular entertainment in Peru help define its culture—the beliefs, customs, and ways of life that make Peru unique.

Art Before the Spanish

Some of the earliest examples of great Peruvian art date to the Chavín, who lived along the coast about three thousand years ago. Their artists created stone sculptures of animals and spirits. They also created pottery. The Moche, who followed the Chavín, made pottery that featured detailed, lifelike images of both animals and people. They, like other peoples who followed them, were also skilled metalworkers, particularly with gold.

The Incas copied many of the artistic styles that existed throughout Peru and made some items on large scale. The remains of some of their massive buildings show their skill working with stone. They also sculpted stone to decorate important religious sites. Textiles were more than fabric used to make clothes. The color and patterns on cloth could indicate a person's social importance or reflect religious beliefs.

The Moche people were highly skilled potters. They made water jars in a wide array of forms, including portraits of individuals and people performing everyday activities. They also made them in the shape of animals such as owls, jaguars, and sea lions.

A Lasting Play

The Incas and other indigenous people of Peru did not have written languages. As a result, they did not have written stories, but they were able to pass on stories by telling them. Some people think a play from Peru's colonial times performed in the Quechua language is based on an earlier Incan tale. *Ollantay* tells the story of an Incan general (left) who is forbidden to marry the princess he loves. The first written version of the play appeared in the 1770s, thanks to a Spanish priest. He may have copied a story he heard from the Incas, or he may have changed the story a bit. Some people say the priest may have made it up. In any case, the play keeps alive a part of Incan culture, and it is still performed today.

Today, the descendants of the Incas and earlier peoples of Peru still practice their traditional art forms. Peruvian textiles and ceramics use some of the same patterns found on art made centuries ago.

European Influence

The Spanish brought with them artistic styles that developed in Europe. Figures of saints and other religious images were a key part of colonial art. A style of painting known as the Cusco school blended European images with some indigenous styles and subjects. For example, in one painting of the Last Supper, Jesus and his disciples are eating guinea pig, a common Incan food.

By the nineteenth century, painters in Peru were turning away from religious topics. The artist Pancho Fierro was known for watercolors showing scenes of everyday life in Peru. In the twentieth century, more painters chose to focus on indigenous people and their culture. Leading this movement was José Sabogal, who often painted portraits of indigenous people in traditional clothing.

One of Peru's best-known artists of recent years is Víctor Delfín. Both a painter and a sculptor, he uses materials such as wood and aluminum. In the 1990s, Delfín organized other artists to speak out against the harsh rule of Alberto Fujimori.

Víctor Delfín works on a painting in his studio.

Visitors who want to see the long and rich history of Peruvian art head to the Museum of Art of Lima. The more than seventeen thousand pieces of art there include three-thousand-year-old artifacts, Spanish colonial art, and modern works. About 1,200 works are always on display, and the museum also has special exhibitions. Its collection includes furniture, ceramics, and textiles along with paintings and photographs. The museum opened in 1961, but the building itself dates to 1872. One of the designers of the building was Gustave Eiffel, who is most famous for building the Eiffel Tower in Paris.

The Written Word

While the Incas did not have a writing system, they did record information on knotted strings called *quipu*. Both numbers and stories were recorded in this way. Runners could then carry the information across the empire.

The Spanish brought a written language to Peru and helped create written versions of Quechua and other indigenous languages. The Spanish also produced the first written histories of Peru, starting with their conquest and the history of the Incas as they learned it from local sources. Indigenous and mestizo writers also wrote on these topics. The native writer Felipe Guaman Poma de Ayala produced a long account of the way Spanish officials destroyed the local culture.

After independence and into the twentieth century, some Peruvian writers copied styles of poetry and fiction writing that were popular in Europe. Some of the first writers to win international notice were the poet César Vallejo and Julio Ramón Ribeyro, who wrote stories and plays. Both writers had their works translated into English. Ribeyro's best-known work, *Chronicle of San Gabriel*, tells the story of a Lima teenager who is sent to live in a rural community.

In recent years, Daniel Alarcón has won praise for his work written in English, though he considers himself a Latin

Between 1600 and 1615, Felipe Guaman Poma de Ayala wrote a book about the Spanish invasion of Peru. Over a thousand pages long, it included hundreds of drawings, such as this one that shows an Incan town with a suspended bridge.

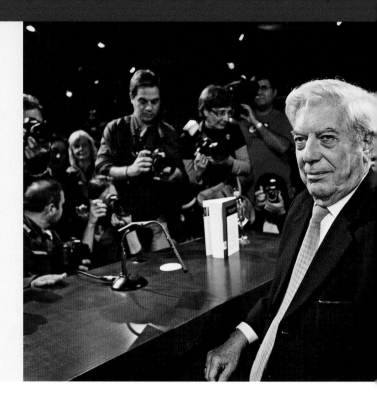

A Prize-Winning Peruvian

Peru's best-known writer is Mario Vargas Llosa. Born in Arequipa in 1936, he spent some of his early years in Bolivia before his family moved to Lima. In college, he studied both literature and law. Vargas Llosa wrote plays, stories, and newspaper articles before writing his first novel, *The City and the Dogs* (also published as *The Time of the Hero*), in 1963. His books often deal with political and social issues in Peru, though sometimes he includes elements of his own life, as in *Aunt Julia and the Scriptwriter*. He also wrote several books set in the jungles of Peru. In 1990, Vargas Llosa ran for president of Peru but lost. In 2010, he received the Nobel Prize in Literature, the world's highest honor for a writer.

American writer. Some of his writing is set in Peru. He also does a Spanish-language podcast on events in Latin America. In 2010, he worked with the Peruvian artist Sheila Alvarado to create the graphic novel *City of Clowns*.

Music Everywhere

Music was an important part of Incan society, and it remains important in Peru today. The Incas played music during all sorts of festivals and religious ceremonies, and soldiers went into battle singing songs. Their main instruments were drums and different kinds of wind instruments. One wind instrument, known today as the *zampoña*, has bamboo pipes of different lengths tied together. These panpipes, as they're often called, are still an important part of music for indigenous people in the Andes. Groups of Andean musicians also

bring their pipes and drums to cities around the world. The Andean style can be heard in the Peruvian song "El Condor Pasa" ("The Condor Flies Past"), which has been recorded by several American musicians.

The Spanish introduced the guitar and other stringed instruments to Peru, and that instrument remains an important part of the country's music. Another European influence came through the waltz, a dance that developed in Germany hundreds of years ago. Waltzes are often played at parties in the cities.

Africans, both enslaved and free, brought the rhythmic dance music of their native lands to Peru. The Afro-Peruvian style they created is popular among peoples of all backgrounds, and examples of the music have been recorded for international audiences. A style of music called *música criolla*

The zampoña is one of the most common traditional Andean instruments. To play it, the musician holds the pipes vertically and then blows horizontally over the top of them.

Better Lives with Music

In four regions in Peru, children from poor families are learning how to play instruments in a program called Sinfonía por el Perú (Symphony for Peru). People who have studied the young students found that the children do more than make music together. They also improve their image of themselves, do better in school, and have better relations with their families. The program began in 2011 thanks to the efforts of Juan Diego Flórez, a Peruvian opera singer who performs around the world.

combines the Afro-Peruvian influence with both Spanish folk music and Andean music.

Young Peruvians enjoy popular music with roots in North America and Europe, while producing their own versions of these styles. One of the best examples is Lucho Quequezana,

A Special Singer

Susana Baca (1944–) has helped spread Afro-Peruvian music around the world. She grew up in a part of Lima where many other Afro-Peruvians lived. At weekend gatherings, she heard music from across Latin America that was influenced by Africans who settled in the region. Baca worked as a teacher before becoming a singer. She brings many of the musical styles she heard as a child to her performances, along with Afro-Peruvian influences. Baca has won two Grammy awards, and in 2011 she entered the cabinet of President Ollanta Humala as the minister of culture. She was the first black Peruvian to serve in a presidential cabinet.

who created jazz using traditional Peruvian instruments. His 2014 record *Combi* was nominated for a Grammy Award, one of the top music awards in the world. The band Novalima blends Afro-Peruvian musical styles with electronic dance music.

Film and Television

Peruvians have been making movies since the early days of silent films shot in black and white. Few people outside the country, however, saw films made in Peru until recent decades. The country's first widely known filmmaker was Armando Robles Godoy, who was born in New York but moved to Peru when he was a boy. His best-known work is the 1970 film *La Muralla Verde* (*The Green Wall*), which won prizes at film festivals around the world. In recent years, Claudia Llosa has won acclaim for her movies *Madeinusa* and *La Teta Asustada* (*The Milk of Sorrow*), which was nominated for the Best Foreign Film at the 2010 Academy Awards.

In television, a 2008 show produced in Peru called *Mi Problema con las Mujeres* (*My Problem with Women*) became popular across the country. Shows based on the program appeared in several other countries.

Silvana Arias is a television actress born in Lima who started her career in her home country. For several years in the early 2000s she was part of the cast on a U.S. soap opera. Stephanie Cayo took a similar path, acting on Peruvian TV as a child before starring on shows in Colombia. In 2015, she filmed a Spanish-language show for the U.S. company Netflix. Cayo is also a popular singer.

Staying Active

Sports provide popular entertainment for many Peruvians, who enjoy playing as well as watching. The top sport in the country is soccer. Lima has two major professional soccer teams. The whole country unites to support the national team when it plays in international events.

Many Peruvians also closely follow the women's national volleyball team, which at its peak during the 1980s won an Olympic medal and a world championship. The team remains one of the best in South America.

Claudia Llosa won the Golden Bear award for best film at the 2009 Berlin Film Festival for *The Milk of Sorrow*.

In Lima, bullfighting is a popular sport. Some people oppose it, however, because of the violence directed against the bulls.

Along the coast, especially in the north, many Peruvians enjoy surfing. Inland, some people try their hand at sandboarding, using small surfboards to sail down huge sand dunes.

Sandboarding down a huge dune can be just as thrilling as snowboarding down a mountain.

Peru's Best

Peru's national soccer team has existed for almost one hundred years, but no one has ever scored more goals for the team than Paolo Guerrero (1984–). After playing professionally in Peru, Guerrero played eight years in Europe before joining a team in Brazil in 2015. That year, he led the league in goals. By 2017, he was considered one of the world's best strikers—a player whose main job is to score goals.

CHAPTER 10

Families and Friends

PERU IS A DIVERSE LAND, AND THE DAILY LIFE OF THE people reflects that. The gap between Peru's wealthiest and poorest citizens also affects how people live. People with good jobs in the coastal cities have lives filled with modern conveniences. But in poor urban neighborhoods, the remote parts of the Andes, and in the Amazon, some people struggle to have clean water to drink. About 10 percent of Peru's population lives on just over $3 per day.

Whatever social class people come from, spending time with family is important to most Peruvians. People also enjoy themselves on weekends and holidays. Many of the country's festivals involve religious celebrations. Food is always a part of celebrations, with most regions having their own special dishes.

Opposite: **Boys in Lima. About 26 percent of Peruvians are under age fifteen.**

What's in a Name?

Peruvians, like many people in Spanish-speaking lands, often have two last names. The second-to-last name comes from the father's family name, and the last one comes from the mother's family name. In practice, though, just the father's last name is commonly used for the children's last name. When they get married, most women do not take on either of their husband's last names.

A Typical Day

For people in Lima and other cities, the workday starts fairly early. People eat a light breakfast of bread and coffee before heading out. Office work usually starts around 8:30 a.m., with a two-hour break for lunch around noon. Long lunches are common throughout South America. In Peru, fewer people go home for lunch than in the past. Most have a meal at a restaurant, and it's often the biggest meal of the day. A 2015 study found that about one-third of all Peruvians work forty-eight hours or more per week. The workday ends around 6:00 p.m., and the evening meal starts at 7:00 p.m. or even later.

Many urban families hire someone to help them do chores. Most common is a woman called a *muchacha*. In the past these helpers often lived with the families, but more of them now commute to their jobs. Wealthier families might also hire a nanny to help raise small children. Some grandparents live with their children and help take care of the grandchildren.

Life is harder for the poor who live in the cities. Many settle in what are called *pueblos jóvenes*—"young towns"—on the outer edges of the cities. In these areas, housing is often simple shacks, and some people have no home at all. Getting clean water can be hard, too. In recent years, though, some of the older pueblos jóvenes have seen some improvement. They have paved roads and reliable sources of water.

People who live in these outer areas around Peru's cities might have to travel several hours each way to get to and from work. Many work in what is called the informal economy— they sell food or small items on the street. Many women and young people work at these jobs, and some have two or three different jobs.

A Peruvian boy poses with his father and grandfather.

The Homes of Peru

Housing in Peru often reflects local climates and the kind of building material available. Adobe is often used in the Andes and in some coastal areas. Thick adobe walls help keep homes cool during warm seasons and warm during cool nights. In the Amazon, homes are often built on stilts above water or marshland. They often have roofs made from local plants and large openings instead of walls to let in breezes. In the cities, many homes are made out of brick and concrete, and tall apartment buildings are common. The wealthiest residents of Lima may have second homes along the beach or in the hills outside the city.

For the remote peoples of the Amazon, hunting and fishing for food take up much of their time, along with farming. Some travel by boat to sell extra food in larger towns.

Andean Clothing

If you go to Lima or another large city in Peru, you'll likely see the same kind of clothing North Americans wear. But in the Andes, colorful clothing made from cotton and wool resembles styles that the Incas wore centuries ago. Women are more likely than men to wear this traditional clothing. It includes a wool jacket called a *jobona* and a black skirt called a *pollera*, which often has a colorful band of cloth around its bottom. Over their shoulders, the women wear capes called *mantas*, which they fasten with a pin or by tying together two corners of the cape. The traditional hat is called a *montera*. It can come in different styles, but it typically has a strap that ties around the woman's chin.

Life for the Young

The Peruvian government provides free education across the country and requires students to go to school from ages five through sixteen. The school year runs from March to December. In parts of the country, however, students often don't finish this schooling, because their families need them to work. Girls help out with chores around the home or help raise younger children. In farming areas, boys work with their fathers. Some children also leave their homes to take jobs. In recent years, as many as one-third of the country's children between the ages of five and seventeen were working. But even in poor areas, parents try to make sure their young children receive some schooling. About 95 percent of the population age fifteen and over can read and write.

Students in Lima walk home at the end of the school day. Many schools in Peru require uniforms.

Aim for the Toad

A popular game played in Peru is *sapo*. The name is Spanish for *toad*. A metal toad with an open mouth sits in the middle of a raised wooden board. All around the toad are holes that are given different point values. The aim of the game is to score points by throwing small metal disks into the toad's mouth or the holes. The player with the most points wins. Children typically stand about 10 feet (3 m) away from the board, while adults stand farther back. Legend says that the game is based on an Incan story. People would try to throw gold coins into the mouth of a magical frog that lived in Lake Titicaca. If they hit the target, the frog would grant them a wish.

Although Peru has public education, most families that can afford it pay for private schooling. In both school systems, students take the same courses, as outlined by the government. Required courses include math, science, and art. Older students also study history and English. In private schools, English is used daily along with Spanish. In high school, students can choose to attend a school that teaches technical skills. Peru also has more than one hundred universities.

Time for Fun

When Peruvians are not at school or work, they enjoy spending time with their family. That includes grandparents, aunts, uncles, and cousins. Activities might include sharing meals or going to the beach. Families also get together to celebrate special occasions such as weddings and the many national and religious holidays that take place in Peru.

National Holidays

New Year's Day	January 1
Maundy Thursday	March or April
Good Friday	March or April
Easter Sunday	March or April
Labor Day/May Day	May 1
St. Peter and St. Paul Day	June 29
Independence Day	July 28 and 29
St. Rosa of Lima Day	August 30
Battle of Angamos	October 8
All Saints' Day	November 1
Feast of the Immaculate Conception	December 8
Christmas	December 25

Peru's diversity is reflected in its foods. In some regions, fish is a major part of many meals, while meat-based soups are common in the Andes. Different roasted meats, such as goat, chicken, and pork, are popular across Peru. Potatoes are eaten

A Popular Dish

At fancy restaurants and street-side stands, people in many parts of Peru enjoy their *cuy*. Cuy is the name for guinea pig, and it's been a popular meat since people in the Andes domesticated the rodents about five thousand years ago. Cuy is sometimes served whole—from head to toes—after being roasted or fried. In some Lima restaurants, chefs use the meat instead of fish or other ingredients. The taste has been called a mixture of chicken and rabbit. Some regions of Peru, especially in the Andes, have restaurants called *cuyerias* that specialize in the dish.

everywhere in a variety of ways. A dish called *ocopa* features potatoes covered in a peanut sauce, while *papa rellena* mixes

Peru's National Drink

Across Peru, visitors are bound to see people drinking a fizzy, yellow beverage called Inca Kola. The family who created this popular soft drink was headed by Joseph Robinson Lindley and Martha Lindley, immigrants from England. Settling in Lima, the Lindleys made and sold drinks with carbonation—the bubbles found in drinks such as Coca-Cola. In 1935, the Lindleys' company created Inca Kola, which is flavored with an herb called lemon verbena. U.S. companies like the Coca-Cola Company tried to outsell Inca Kola, but most Peruvians preferred a drink made in their own country. The Lindleys' son Isaac took over the company from his parents and made Inca Kola the most popular soft drink in Peru. Now, the company works with Coca-Cola, which sells Inca Kola in the United States.

mashed potatoes, vegetables, and meat and is then deep-fried. Foods once found mostly in the Amazon region are now turning up in other parts of the country. These include river fish and yucca, which comes from the cassava plant. A popular dessert is *suspiro limeño*, which combines caramel with meringue.

When dining out, Peruvians can also choose to visit a *chifa*, the name for a Chinese restaurant. Lima alone has about six thousand chifas. While they serve typical Chinese food, some also blend in traditional Peruvian ingredients, such as *cuy*—guinea pig. Entertainment outside the home might also include stopping at a *peña*, a small nightclub. Musicians typically play folk music, and audience members might even take a turn performing.

Some of the most important social gatherings in Peru center on religious holidays. One celebration before the start of the

Papa rellena **means "stuffed potato" in English. It is one of the most popular dishes in Peru.**

The Carnaval celebration in Cajamarca gets wild, with people smearing each other with a mix of water, flour, and paint.

Easter season is Carnaval. It features parades and parties before Lent, a somber period that leads up to Easter. One tradition during Carnaval is to throw water balloons or find other ways to soak unsuspecting people. Along with the national religious

An Andean Wedding

Wedding customs in Peru vary. A wedding in Lima might be very similar to one in most parts of North America. But in the Andes, weddings typically last three days or more. In some villages, weddings only occur during one month of the year. On the first night of a particular couple's wedding, their families meet to plan the events that will follow as they share a meal. On the second day, the bride and groom have the official wedding ceremony, followed by a celebration with food, music, and dancing. On the next day, the couple and their families continue to celebrate at the groom's home, with guests coming by with gifts.

holidays, towns also honor individual saints that are special to them. On these feast days, people who have moved to the cities sometimes return to their hometowns or villages to celebrate with friends.

As in many Spanish-speaking lands, one special day for Peruvian girls is their fifteenth birthday. Known as *quinceañera*, the day marks a girl's entry into adulthood. The birthday girl typically wears a long dress, and her family throws a large party with food and music. Some of the celebrations can be as fancy as weddings.

No matter what the occasion, Peruvians love to come together to share good times with family and friends.

A mother in Lima takes a picture of her daughter dressed up for her quinceañera.

Timeline

Peruvian History		World History	
People from Asia begin to settle in Peru.	ca. 11,000 BCE		
The Chavín culture develops.	ca. 1000 BCE		
		ca. 2500 BCE	The Egyptians build the pyramids and the Sphinx in Giza.
		ca. 563 BCE	The Buddha is born in India.
		313 CE	The Roman emperor Constantine legalizes Christianity.
		610	The Prophet Muhammad begins preaching a new religion called Islam.
		1054	The Eastern (Orthodox) and Western (Roman Catholic) Churches break apart.
		1095	The Crusades begin.
The Incas appear in the valley near Cusco.	1200s CE	1215	King John seals the Magna Carta.
The Chimú build the city of Chan Chan.	ca. 1300	1300s	The Renaissance begins in Italy.
The Inca Empire expands.	1400s	1347	The plague sweeps through Europe.
		1453	Ottoman Turks capture Constantinople, conquering the Byzantine Empire.
		1492	Columbus arrives in North America.
Spanish conquistadores led by Francisco Pizarro defeat the Incas.	1532	1500s	Reformers break away from the Catholic Church, and Protestantism is born.
The Spanish establish their capital in Lima.	1535		
The Spanish kill Túpac Amaru, the last Incan king.	1572		
An earthquake destroys much of Lima.	1746		

PERUVIAN HISTORY

Túpac Amaru II leads a rebellion against the Spanish.	**1780**
Peru declares its independence from Spain.	**1821**
Peru, Chile, and Bolivia fight the War of the Pacific.	**1879–1883**
Peru sends about 2,200 Japanese-Peruvians to the United States.	**1942**
An earthquake centered in Chimbote kills seventy thousand people.	**1970**
The rebel group Shining Path terrorizes Peru.	**1980s**
Alberto Fujimori is elected president and greatly weakens the Shining Path.	**1990**
Author Mario Vargas Llosa wins the Nobel Prize in Literature.	**2010**
Pedro Pablo Kuczynski is elected president.	**2016**
Heavy flooding kills more than one hundred people.	**2017**

WORLD HISTORY

1776	The U.S. Declaration of Independence is signed.
1789	The French Revolution begins.
1865	The American Civil War ends.
1879	The first practical lightbulb is invented.
1914	World War I begins.
1917	The Bolshevik Revolution brings communism to Russia.
1929	A worldwide economic depression begins.
1939	World War II begins.
1945	World War II ends.
1969	Humans land on the Moon.
1975	The Vietnam War ends.
1989	The Berlin Wall is torn down as communism crumbles in Eastern Europe.
1991	The Soviet Union breaks into separate states.
2001	Terrorists attack the World Trade Center in New York City and the Pentagon near Washington, D.C.
2004	A tsunami in the Indian Ocean destroys coastlines in Africa, India, and Southeast Asia.
2008	The United States elects its first African American president.
2016	Donald Trump is elected U.S. president.

Timeline **129**

Fast Facts

Official name: Republic of Peru

Capital: Lima

Official languages: Spanish, Quechua, Aymara

Lima

National flag

Paracas Peninsula

Official religion:	None
Founding date:	July 28, 1821, independence from Spain
National anthem:	"Himno Nacional del Perú" ("National Anthem of Peru")
Type of government:	Republic
Head of state:	President
Head of government:	President
Area:	496,224 square miles (1,285,214 sq km)
Geographic center:	10° S, 76° W
Bordering countries:	Ecuador and Colombia to the north, Brazil and Bolivia to the east, Chile to the south
Highest elevation:	Huascarán, 22,205 feet (6,768 m) above sea level
Lowest elevation:	Bayóvar Depression, 111 feet (34 m) below sea level
Average daily high temperature:	In Lima, 82°F (28°C) in February, 66°F (19°C) in July; in Cusco, 64.5°F (18°C) in February, 64.5°F (18°C) in July
Average daily low temperature:	In Lima, 65°F (18.5°C) in February, 54°F (12°C) in July; in Cusco, 43°F (6°C) in February, 32°F (0°C) in July
Average annual precipitation:	Varies, from 0.3 inches (0.8 cm) in Lima to 198 inches (503 cm) in Quince Mil

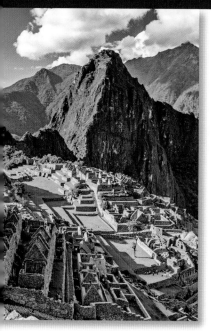

Machu Picchu

National population (2017 est.): 32,172,457

Population of major cities (2017 est.):

Lima	7,737,002
Arequipa	841,130
Callao	813,264
Trujillo	747,450
Chiclayo	577,375

Landmarks:
- ▶ *Chan Chan*, near Trujillo
- ▶ *Floating islands*, Lake Titicaca
- ▶ *Machu Picchu*, Cusco region
- ▶ *Manú National Park*, near Cusco
- ▶ *Nazca Lines*, Nazca

Economy: Peru has large reserves of many important minerals. It is the world's third-largest producer of copper and is also a major supplier of silver, gold, and zinc, among other metals. Peruvian fishers catch fish eaten around the world and also haul in anchovies, which are often used for fish meal. Crops grown for export include asparagus, artichokes, and quinoa. Important manufactured goods include cement, textiles, and products made from petroleum. Services make up the largest part of Peru's economy. Important service sectors include government, education, financial services, and tourism.

Currency: Nuevo sol. In 2017, 1 sol equaled US$0.31, and US$1.00 equaled 3.25 soles.

System of weights and measures: Metric system

Literacy rate: 95%

Currency

Teacher and student

Susana Baca

Common Spanish words and phrases:

Por favor	Please
Sí	yes
No	no
Hola	Hello
Gracias	Thank you
De nada	You're welcome
Buenos días	Good morning
Adiós	Good-bye
¿Cómo está?	How are you?
Muy bien	very well

Prominent Peruvians:

Túpac Amaru (ca. 1540–1572)
Incan king

Susana Baca (1944–)
Singer

Micaela Bastidas (ca. 1741–1781)
Rebel leader

Víctor Delfín (1927–)
Artist

Martin de Porres (1579–1639)
Saint

Miguel Grau (1834–1879)
Admiral

Paolo Guerrero (1984–)
Soccer player

Julio C. Tello (1880–1947)
Archaeologist

Mario Vargas Llosa (1936–)
Nobel Prize–winning writer

To Find Out More

Books

▶ Bjorklund, Ruth. *Peru*. New York: Cavendish Square, 2017.

▶ Burgan, Michael. *Ancient Incas*. New York: Children's Press, 2013.

▶ Jackson, Tom. *The Amazon*. London: Dorling Kindersley, 2015.

▶ Toledo, Daniel. *Francisco Pizarro: Conqueror of the Incan Empire*. New York: Rosen Publishing, 2017.

▶ Weitzman, Elizabeth. *Mysteries of Machu Picchu*. Minneapolis: Lerner Publications, 2017.

Videos

▶ *Machu Picchu*. London: Atlantic Productions, 2016.

▶ *Peru: An Ancient Land*. New York: International Masters Publishers, 2011.

▶ *Planet Food Collection: Peru*. London: Pilot Productions, 2013.

▶ Visit this Scholastic website for more information on Peru:
www.factsfornow.scholastic.com
Enter the keyword Peru

Index

Page numbers in *italics*
indicate illustrations.

Meet the Author

MICHAEL BURGAN HAS ALWAYS been fascinated by history and geography, and he has been able to combine those interests writing for the Enchantment of the World series. Peru is the sixth country he's examined for the series. His earlier books were on Chile, Kenya, the United States, Belgium, and Malaysia. He also previously wrote a book about the Incas. Over his career, Burgan has written more than 250 books for children and teens, most of them about history or geography.

He graduated from the University of Connecticut with a degree in history. In his free time, he writes plays and enjoys traveling and taking pictures. He is also editor of *The Biographer's Craft*, the monthly newsletter for Biographers International Organization (BIO). He lives in Santa Fe, New Mexico, with his cat, Callie.

Photo Credits

Photographs ©:

cover: Grant Faint/Getty Images; back cover: Christian Heeb/AWL Images; 2: SteveAllenPhoto/iStockphoto; 5: Danita Delimont Stock/AWL Images; 6 left: Nigel Pavitt/Getty Images; 6 right: Ricardo Ribas/Alamy Images; 6 center: hadynyah/iStockphoto; 7 left: danbreckwoldt/iStockphoto; 7 right: Morales/age fotostock; 8: rest/iStockphoto; 11: Hemis/Alamy Images; 12: Beata Bernina/Getty Images; 13: Bill Bachmann/age fotostock; 14: Christian Ender/Getty Images; 15: Jeff Greenberg/age fotostock; 16: José Enrique Molina/age fotostock; 18: Derek Trask/Alamy Images; 19 top: Beataaldridge/Dreamstime; 19 bottom: Jason Langley/Alamy Images; 20 left: Sandra Salvadó/age fotostock; 21: F. Neukirchen/age fotostock; 22 top: Richard Roscoe/Barcroft Images/Getty Images; 22 bottom: danbreckwoldt/iStockphoto; 23: Chris Cheadle/age fotostock; 24: ERNESTO BENAVIDES/AFP/Getty Images; 25: Prisma by Dukas Presseagentur GmbH/Alamy Images; 26: Gabby Salazar/Getty Images; 27 top: PATRICIA LACHIRA/AFP/Getty Images; 27 bottom: Pawel Bienkowski/Alamy Images; 28: Morales/age fotostock; 30: Juan Manuel Borrero/Album/Superstock, Inc.; 31 top: Mark Tunstall/Dreamstime; 31 bottom: Mark Bowler/Getty Images; 32: marktucan/Shutterstock; 33: Pixattitude/Dreamstime; 34 top: Dirk Ercken/Dreamstime; 34 bottom: byllwill/Getty Images; 35: Naturepix/Alamy Images; 36: Vladimir Cech/Dreamstime; 37: Mint Frans Lanting/age fotostock; 38 bottom: Nigel Pavitt/Getty Images; 38 top: Robert Wyatt/Alamy Images; 39: Wigbert Röth/imageBROKER/age fotostock; 40: Nathan Benn/Corbis/Getty Images; 42: Regina Siebrecht/Getty Images; 43: MARTIN BERNETTI/AFP/Getty Images; 44: Chrishowey/Dreamstime; 45: Stock Connection Blue/Alamy Images; 47: Siempreverde22/iStockphoto; 48: PRISMA ARCHIVO/Alamy Images; 49: DEA/G DAGLI ORTI/age fotostock; 50: Double wedding between two Inca women and two Spaniards in 1558, c.1750 (panel), Spanish School, (18th century)/Nuestra Senora de Copacabana, Lima, Peru/Bridgeman Art Library; 51: Werner Forman Archive/age fotostock; 53: The Print Collector/age fotostock; 54: DEA/M SEEMULLER/age fotostock; 55: DEA/M SEEMULLER/age fotostock; 56: Bettmann/Getty Images; 57: Paul Fearn/Alamy Images; 59: Oktay Ortakcioglu/iStockphoto; 60: MIGUEL BELLIDO /EL COMERCIO /GDA/AP Images; 61: DANTE ZEGARRA/AFP/Getty Images; 62: Charles O. Cecil/Alamy Images; 64: LINO CHIPANA/EL COMERCIO/GDA/AP Images; 65 top: Christian Vinces/Shutterstock; 66 top: JUAN PONCE VALENZUELA/GDA/AP Images; 66 bottom: Gil C/Shutterstock; 67: Ernesto Arias/EFE News Agency/Alamy Images; 68: CRIS BOURONCLE/AFP/Getty Images; 69: Marco del Rio /LatinContent/Getty Images; 70: Robert Fried/Alamy Images; 72: Florian Kopp/imageBROKER/age fotostock; 73: PA Images/Alamy Images; 74: Keren Su/China Span/Alamy Images; 76: José Enrique Molina/age fotostock; 78: Florian Kopp/imageBROKER/age fotostock; 79: Sebastian Castañeda/Anadolu Agency/Getty Images; 80 top: Serjio74/iStockphoto; 80 bottom: age fotostock/Alamy Images; 81: CRIS BOURONCLE/AFP/Getty Images; 82: Ulita/Dreamstime; 83: Chatursunil/Dreamstime; 84: Blaine Harrington III/Alamy Images; 87: Frances Roberts/Alamy Images; 89: Kaszojad/iStockphoto; 90: Mike Goldwater/Alamy Images; 91 top: VWPics/AP Images; 91 bottom: Aurora Photos/Alamy Images; 92: Jean-Paul Van Belle; 93: Rodrigo Abd/AP Images; 94: Renato Granieri/Alamy Images; 96: Carlos Mora/Alamy Images; 97: HUGHES Herv/hemis f/age fotostock; 98: STEPHEN ALVAREZ/National Geographic Creative; 99 top: torukojin/iStockphoto; 99 bottom: PocholoCalapre/iStockphoto; 100: Albin Lohr-Jones/Pacific Press/LightRocket/Getty Images; 101: Domenico Stinellis/AP Images; 102: South America/Alamy Images; 104: Carlosphotos/Dreamstime; 105: Nathan Benn/Corbis/Getty Images; 106: Jim Dyson/Getty Images; 107: Federico Tovoli/VWPics/age fotostock; 108: CRIS BOURONCLE/AFP/Getty Images; 109: DEA/G. DAGLI ORTI/Getty Images; 110: Jose Miguel Alfonso/age fotostock; 111: Radu Razvan Gheorghe/Dreamstime; 112 top: CRIS BOURONCLE/AFP/Getty Images; 112 bottom: Al Pereira/WireImage/Getty Images; 114: Sean Gallup/Getty Images; 115 top: Ricardo Ribas/Alamy Images; 115 bottom: Buda Mendes/Getty Images; 116: Florian Kopp/imageBROKER/age fotostock; 119: Jeff Greenberg/age fotostock; 120 top: Nigel J.H. Smith/age fotostock; 120 bottom: hadynyah/iStockphoto; 121: Mirek Nowaczyk/Shutterstock; 122: Mircea Nicolescu/Dreamstime; 123: CRIS BOURONCLE/AFP/Getty Images; 124 top: ManuelGonzalezOlaecheaFranco/iStockphoto; 124 bottom: FrankvandenBergh/iStockphoto; 125: Robert Lerich/Dreamstime; 126 top: Carlos Mora/Alamy Images; 126 bottom: James Brunker/Alamy Images; 127: RosaIreneBetancourt 3/Alamy Images; 130 left: Christian Vinces/Shutterstock; 131 top: Gil C/Shutterstock; 131 bottom: José Enrique Molina/age fotostock; 132 bottom: Serjio74/iStockphoto; 132 top: Siempreverde22/iStockphoto; 133 bottom: Al Pereira/WireImage/Getty Images; 133 top: Florian Kopp/imageBROKER/age fotostock.

Maps by Mapping Specialists.